THE
GREAT BRITISH
RAILWAY STATION

KINGS CROSS

By

Chris Hawkins

**IRWELL
PRESS**

The Cross, glittering at night. The oft-bemoaned clutter at its base (known to railwaymen usually as 'the native village') changed, grew and shrank over the years but on occasion at least Cubitt's great screen could rise above almost anything. Here it basks in the new and hopeful blaze of Nationalisation though by day or night it represented a classic contrast of stern simplicity and muddled afterthought. It was probably fitting in a sense that the ground in front of the famous Italianate screen should ever afterwards be considered squalid; the place after all had hardly been salubrious even before the arrival of the 'Permanent Passenger Station' and was 'little more than a gigantic dustyard' in 1850, in the shadow of the nearby Fever Hospital. This was pulled down and buildings filled all the land about. Medcalf (see later) was at his best in describing these prehistoric days for he had after all begun his service 'in the temporary station in York Road', that is York Way/Maiden Lane: 'The Great Northern had got hold of the waste, howling wilderness for their London terminus and soon a clean sweep in a very complete sense was made and the plain straightforward solid brickwork of the station arose to dominate Kings Cross.' The place was a meeting of several roads by 1850, coming together rather to the east of the station where Maiden Lane (York Road, later York Way) came due south along the east side of the terminus. Maiden Lane (it lays off to the far right in this view) became 'John Street' at this point and in the crude 'circus' between it and Grays Inn Road and the rest stood 'an obelisk'. A point 'below the top of the obelisk at Kings Cross London' provided a datum reference for the driving of the Great Northern tunnels. For almost twenty years the Cubitt screen fronted the road itself but alterations consequent upon the erection of St. Pancras left an open space.

(Camden Libraries)

Published by

Irwell Press

3 Durley Avenue, Pinner, Middlesex, HA5 1JQ.

Printed by Amadeus Press, Huddersfield

The Kings Cross roof girders had originally been of 'laminated timber' and accounts of the station drew attention to its later replacement in steel. Medcalf, latterly the Kings Cross Goods Manager (one of the principal commercial positions of the Great Northern) could actually recall the doubts expressed about such a method: the girders might 'relieve their own extreme tension by crudely straining the outer walls in which they were socketed'. The offices on the western side would obviate this it was thought, but the east side (on the left here) was considered more at risk.

(National Railway Museum)

Contents

Muddle at The Cross in British Railways days. The 'howling waste' of its frontage had indeed seen some widely differing times. A locomotive passed through the forecourt in 1860 to land in the debris of the Metropolitan Railway construction works whilst in the first years the front had been open and spacious. Before the 'ugly encroachments of temporary huts and underground stations to spoil ones views', it was a place ... 'of bustle and brightness but without noise'. ... 'LR' in The LNER Magazine lamented the difference then and now: 'How different the scene which greets one today. There is no open and spacious forecourt in which a troop of horses could prance, but what seems almost like a back entrance into the station. Certainly the way in is not obvious from the main road. The buildings in front have done their job well, if that job was to hide the one beautiful piece of architecture at King's Cross, the station frontage. Where ladies and their beaux promenaded one has to skip away from oncoming taxis and inter-station buses, with their semi-top decks and notices about boat trains.' 'LR' looked back to when ladies in crinolines with their young men on York Race days strolled unhurriedly to the trains, horse drawn buses from Bank and High Holborn called outside and a 'troop of Horse Guards in their gay uniforms and plumed helmets' might also be travelling.

(The Thompson Society)

Simple impression of the Kings Cross girdering, the single departure platform on the left, the one arrival platform to the right.

A Howling Waste

Judged by many the greatest of London's stations, Kings Cross has been perhaps the most enduring of the great termini. This despite a mean clutter of buildings jumbled unthinkingly at its feet, two World Wars and successive attempts at reconstruction. The latest proposals – 'the biggest urban renewal project in Western Europe' – is only the latest in a series of threats.

Kings Cross might possibly be the best known station in Britain. Of all our country's *great stations* it is possibly the most likely to spring to the lips even of the uninitiated. Of the four *Monopoly* stations it is the first to be recalled and Kings Cross is possibly alone (though Euston might press it close here) in the public mind as firstly a railway station and only secondly a district. Its austere facade (it is difficult to be wholly original in describing Kings Cross, but that is the term which leaps immediately to mind, amongst a variety of observers) is now the perfect foil to the dreaming Gothic of St Pancras. And herein lies some hope for the verdict our descendants may give upon some less admirable post-war contrasts; the shock tends to lessen over the generations. Both buildings were denigrated over periods but are now artistically unassailable

An obscure district, Kings Cross had already been made unlovely by the sprawling effects of industry and urbanisation, even as the 1850s dawned. The Imperial Gas Works was already open and dismal courts huddled close about. An obelisk marked the centre of an important conjunction of roads – 'Kings Cross' and the Regents Canal lay close by. So, the Parishes of St Pancras and St Mary Islington were areas of contrast, the first ugly stirrings of industry amidst fields already plundered for brick workings. Kilns dotted the place and housing was growing up on the roads leading into the open country of Hornsey and the wilderness beyond. A plan exists at the Public Record Office, signed by Joseph Cubitt (son of Sir William Cubitt, knighted in 1851) labelled 'GNR Kings Cross Passenger station and line extending to junction with main line at Copenhagen Tunnel 1852'. It shows crowded courts on the station site, the Fever Hospital (originally established safely beyond the outskirts of the capital) and the Great Northern main line. In the middle of brickfields, this is pencilled on Cubitt's plan as 'already open'. The site of Kings Cross yard and depot and later, 'Top Shed' were similarly dismal fields. The final link, delving under the Regents Canal, with all its complications, is shown making a junction with the existing line a few yards from the southern portal of Copenhagen Tunnel (scene long after of *The Ladykillers*) and a little east of the tile and brick making village of *Belle Isle*. The deviation limits of the approved route ran close to the margins of the village; it lay on the east side of Maiden Lane (later to form York Way) and the line at first crossed this thoroughfare, to land awkwardly in the middle of damp and open brick fields. It is nice to imagine that these inauspicious beginnings were owed in some small part to the Directors' desire to benefit from the Great Exhibition traffic of 1851; business would flow from this (and, with luck, honours and emolluments for the Directors) and the Engineer was whipped ever on through 1849 and 1850. *The London Temporary Passenger Station* opened amidst the Belle Isle brickfields on August 7th 1850, a few days late; on 6th June 1850 a *Report* had been received from Joseph Cubitt the Engineer ... *upon the apprehended delay in opening the line London – Peterborough till the middle of August and upon the very great importance of steps being taken to ensure it being opened by the 1st August.*

On Thursday 27th September 1849 Joseph Cubitt had reported his attempts *to accelerate the rate of progress of the works between London and Peterborough ... His efforts were rewarded; on 6th December 1849 the Board resolved that he be appointed Architect for the London Temporary Passenger Station and permanent Goods Station, upon condition that his terms are satisfactory to the Station Committee, it being the opinion of the Board that from the extent of the works he ought to charge less than Mr Goddard.*

On Thursday 18th July 1850 Cubitt was pleased to report to his Board that *the London to Peterborough portion of main line will be ready for the inspection of the Directors on the 27th July, and be opened to the Public on Wednesday 7th August next.* This was indeed the opening date of the Great Northern main line, into its (to borrow somewhat from the style of the Minutes) *Temporary Passenger station at Kings Cross.* frequently referred to in the literature as 'Maiden Lane'. Cubitt cut it fine, or his confidence was rewarded; there appears to be no mention of official Government approval for the works, though he records 'Peterborough to Wennington – he presumably means *Werrington* – sanctioned for the public by the Railway Commissioners' on 7th August 1850.

The Directors were concerned principally with costs and rates; dull fare, and there is no account of celebratory fanfares for the opening of the new route. On 6th June 1850 the Board is worrying itself about appointments for the new undertaking. 'Clerks and Guards', it declared, 'should not exceed 30 years of age'. Earlier, in February, it had been resolved 'that the Executive Committee do reconsider the question of the proposed widening of Maiden Lane with a view to avoid too great an outlay.' This is almost the only reference in these earliest years to Maiden Lane, now York Way; the new line was pushed across it to its lacklustre termination.

This 'Temporary Passenger Station', whatever its precise location, at least had a roof (it afterwards apparently served as potato warehouse) though it appears not to have given every satisfaction. On Thursday 24th October 1850 Lewis Cubitt* attended the Board 'and explained his plans for the roofing for the new station at Kings Cross, which he proposes, instead of that now in use at the Temporary Passenger Station, in consequence of it not being considered safe. Resolved, that his plans be approved and accepted.'

The Directors were much more concerned with revenue, and in particular that accruing from the Great Exhibition, and as Joseph Cubitt prepared to delve and tunnel his great venture under the Regents Canal (the contractors, John and William Jay, were employing upwards of a thousand men) above ground the General Manager proposed the following Exhibition arrangements 'for the month of September:'

York. Up Train Monday and Saturday as at present, at 9.45am

Sheffield. None.

Leeds and Wakefield. Up Train on Monday, Wednesday and Saturday.

Lincoln and Doncaster. Up Train on Monday and Saturday.

Peterborough and the Royston and Hitchin Districts. One train a week, say Thursday, and back on that day or any other Exhibition day.

Down Trains Mondays, Thursdays and Saturdays to Leeds etc. and the two days named above, to York, Doncaster and Lincoln, in order to balance the Scotch Fish Trains which run daily from York (except Sundays) I propose to run daily from Kings Cross to York etc. at 9.15pm. No Exhibition passengers to be carried up or down by ordinary trains.

(sgd)Seymour Clarke

Attention turns more and more to the new 'Permanent Kings Cross' through the latter part of 1851 and into the following year.

Sir William Cubitt 'requested to the Board' on 27th January 1852, *on the state of station buildings ... to the effect that work is now progressing satisfactorily and that no fears need be entertained either of its strength or safety.'*

On Tuesday 30th March after application from the Post Office a letter box 'free of cost and at no expense to the company' was approved for Kings Cross. Opening of the station was not now far off though once again the Board Minutes are strangely indifferent to this great event. 'Mr Joseph Cubitt and Mr Lewis Cubitt' on Tuesday 4th May 1852 were *authorised to come to terms with Mr Jay the Contractor for the station work at Kings Cross in order to gain time for the necessary excavations and cellarage.* On 17th August the General Manager *gave particulars of the arrangements he recommended for working trains into and out of the Permanent Passenger Station at Kings Cross and suggesting that passengers be allowed to alight at the Ticket platform near the Holloway Road and that two cottages for the principal ticket collectors be erected there. Approved.*

Joseph Cubitt wrote on 28th September: *I am proceeding with the completion of the works. I expect another month will bring most of them to conclusion. The wet weather and the unfavourable nature of the material have caused slips both of cuttings and embankments at various points but more particularly at Spittlegate near Grantham, at which place the embankment has caused a good deal of trouble. It is however, now, I believe, effectively cured ... The works of the London Station are likely to be sufficiently completed to be able to open in a fortnight from this time: a great deal of wet weather and considerable difficulty in getting men are the reasons urged from time to time by Mr Jay for greater progress not having been made.*
(sgd)Joseph Cubitt

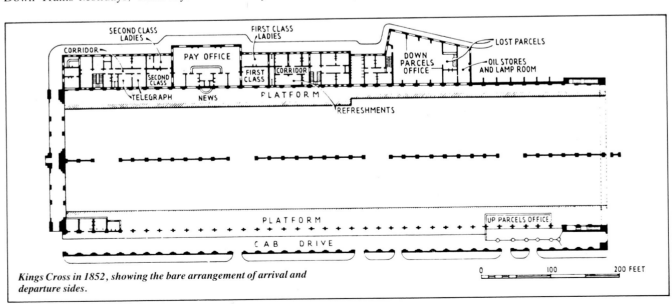

Kings Cross in 1852, showing the bare arrangement of arrival and departure sides.

The Kings Cross terminus had landed in an area of squalor, or at least unpleasantness, and it remained a poorly-off district, down to the present day. Into the 1930s and beyond families lived in verminous single rooms in the streets about and malnourished urchins, frequently bare-footed, abounded in the footways and courtyards. The station seemed ever suited to these surroundings and the buildings at the front of Kings Cross included up to 1902 (of all things — see Jackson, London's Termini) a garden furniture vendors premises. These were burnt out in that year to be succeeded in 1914 by 'the mail office, the Jubilee cloak room, used for heavy parcels, the emigrants transit shed, the excursion office, a timber-built office for railway staff, a cab shelter and plonked right at the front, the 1906 station of the Piccadilly tube railway.' This was the Great Northern Piccadilly and Brompton Railway, in 'standard dark rhubarb terracotta blocks.'

(Camden Libraries)

Even the new station itself failed to evince comment in the Board Minutes — on 12th October 1852 a letter from the Secretary of the Railway Department, Board of Trade, 'conveying the sanction of that Board to the new portion of line and Passenger Station at Kings Cross being opened for Public traffic', was simply 'noted,' and the Directors moved on to tickets, rates, conveyances and solicitors.

'The Great Station' opened on 14th October 1852 and was rightly regarded as architecturally startling, a pair of yawning train sheds bound at first by giant 'laminated timbers', not the girders familiar to the last few generations. Its frontage now ranks foremost amongst the surviving *Great British Stations* and it survived periodic rebuilding proposals from the turn of the century onwards, sometimes by a whisker. In *Notable Railway Stations No. 6*, in a turn of the century *Railway Magazine* account heavily redolent of the official Great Northern view, the station was said to occupy a site that was 'little more than a gigantic dustyard'. Long years of smoke nuisance and other complaint made a snipe at the local authority, what there was of it, irresistible: 'The London County Council was yet in the Womb of Time and even its unlucky predecessor, the Metropolitan Board of Works, had still to be born'. The dismal air of the place prior to the arrival of the Great Northern had lingered long in the corporate memory of the company and J. Medcalf (GN Out Door Goods Manager) recalled it in some style: 'A long battalion of rag sorters and cinder sifters .. the dull heavy thuds of the North London carpet beaters ... the stray cats with wicked propensities ... snapping at a dead sparrow or fighting fiercely with each other over the latest sample of fish bone'.

The Great Northern had 'got hold ... of this howling waste .. and soon made a clean sweep .. the plain straightforward solid brickwork of the station arose to dominate Kings Cross'. Here an element of inferiority begins to creep in .. *according to all precedent we ought to bring in something about the style of architecture but we can't. The broad sweep of the frontage and the fine proportions of the two main arcades are undeniable but the clock tower and one or two other features are not what the dramatic critic would call 'convincing'. The stately Grecian columns of Euston and the ornate Gothic of St. Pancras seem to call across 'what do you call yourself?' and Kings Cross can only reply 'we dont know but we are a big railway station and we are filling the part all the time'.*

Kings Cross then was for much of its time an unregarded building, almost an embarrassment to the Great Northern (which would explain in part its recurring proposals to build upon the area of the frontage) and indeed it settled very quickly into the long banality that is at the heart of every station; Joseph Cubitt occupied the autumn of 1852 with various land purchases for 'Kings Cross Goods' and on 20th October 1852 a cash bag containing more than £60 disappeared overnight from an unlocked drawer at the station.

£14.10s.4d was lost forever but £48 in cheques and bank notes turned up in the post on the 27th. It might even have been posted from the new letter box...

*Lewis Cubitt designed the station itself, Joseph and his father William were responsible for the engineering of the line. Whilst of the same family, Jackson notes in 'London's Termini', 'they were not directly related'.

3

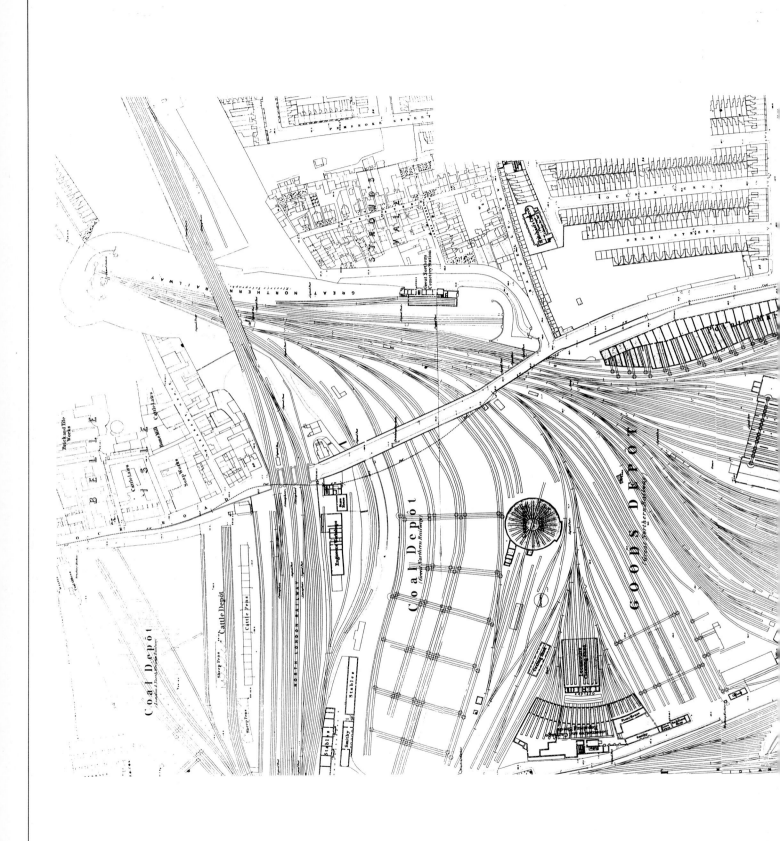

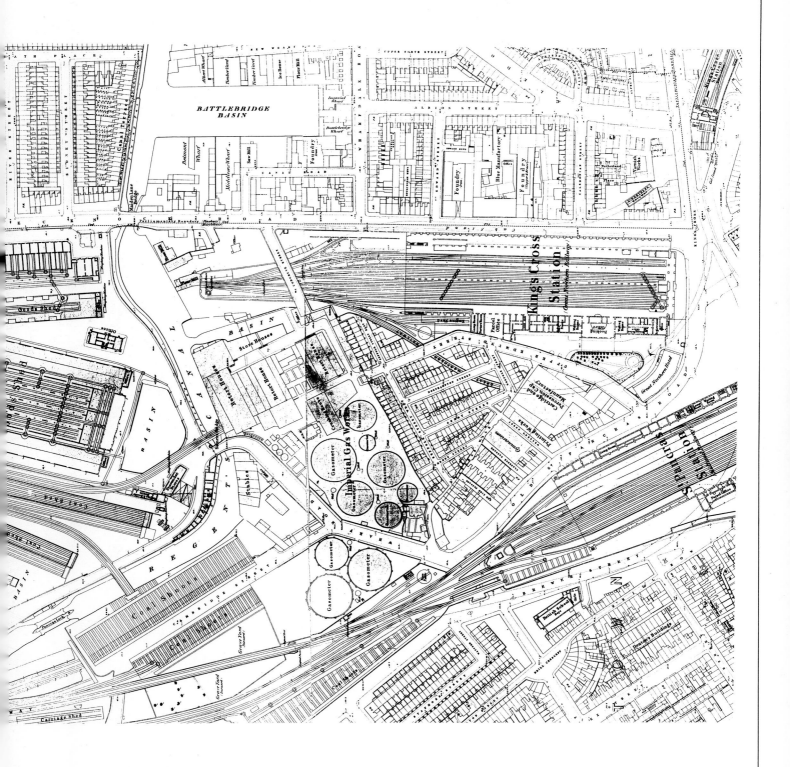

The Cross, from the Ordnance Survey of 1874. The long straight road at the east side of the station has been a bugbear and I've never been quite clear as to the name changes. 'Maiden Lane' it was, at least in its more northerly parts, in the 1850s and by the turn of the century 'York Road' was in frequent use. 'York Way' it always was to us. 'Brecknock Road' is inexplicable except as a map making error. The pub, The Brecknock(the whole area was navigated using pub names – you went 'up Brecknock' or 'down Nag's 'ead', and people knew where you were going) lay a long way off, beyond the Cattle Market. Note Mr. Plimsoll's coal drops – in Cambridge Street. It was always Camley Street and is rendered so in the text.

Tracks & Tunnels

The platforms at Kings Cross varied confusingly over the years; change came of course as the station grew and was re-ordered but an added perversity of logic on the part of the Great Northern made matters even more awkward, labelling the platforms as they appeared over the years in eccentric fashion. Across the wide sweep of the two train sheds, 800ft long, 105ft wide and 71ft* high, 'a vista of extraordinary effect', only two platforms were laid at first, facing each other. The west side, with attendant offices and passengers' rooms, was for departures and the east, or York Way, side, dealt with arrivals only. Between the two stretched no less than fourteen tracks, a standing area for spare and waiting stock, interlinked by the customary arrangement of small turntables, capstans and the like.

The place was jolted out of this pleasantly relaxed working by the arrival of the Midland Railway, in 1858. From 1st February Midland trains ran in from Hitchin, these and the burgeoning Great Northern traffic swiftly rendering the station arrangements inadequate.

Tunnels were delved in the 1860s to connect with the east — west running lines of the Metropolitan Railway. Down trains, leaving the tunnels, emerged from the Widened Lines on the west side of the station — the 'Hotel Curve' and for years simply set back into the terminus for passengers to board or alight. Up trains curved away from the Gas Works Tunnel mouth, to call at a new platform, before diving out of sight in a second single bore, running under York Way for a distance before curving sharply eastwards and uniting with the line through the Hotel Curve, at Metropolitan Junction. New platforms opened in starts on the arrival side of the terminus, serving less than perfectly until departure of the Midland in 1868.

The first 'local lines' at Kings Cross were opened in 1875, two platforms clinging to the west side of the station and closely bounded by a new engine yard. Trains off the Metropolitan continued to set back into these departure platforms until the line up from the depths, on the Hotel Curve, was given its own platform in 1878. In the same year a second Gas Works Tunnel was burrowed out whilst in the previous year a second Copenhagen Tunnel, for goods, had been fashioned, a skew viaduct at its northern end giving independent access from the up lines into the goods yards. The new Gas Works Tunnel stood to the east of the original and necessitated a rebuilt York Road station (on to its latter day site). Of two tracks, like the original, it was devoted to up trains with its predecessor now given over to down workings. It obviously revolutionalised working at the terminus (at long last) and the two tunnels, Gas Works and Copenhagen, were part of a single project, of at least two Contracts; 'No. 2', for 'Kings Cross Additional Tunnel', had been accepted in 1876, at £45,000.

The Gas Works portion ran of course below the Regents Canal and all the work involved the most meticulous planning and foresight. There were a number of features, two coffer dams for the canal, which imply a pumping clear of its waters, 'the station works at York Road' (presumably the new station), and others. These included: 'extension of Congreve Street Bridge on a skew … underpinning potato warehouses in York Road …. Somers Bridge and widening Regents Canal … metalling and draining Frederick Street New Coal

* According to C.A.Johns, One Hundred Years at Kings Cross, but 75ft according to J.Medcalf — Notable Railway Stations, in The Railway Magazine.

Kings Cross in unfamiliar guise, fenced about with brooding bridges; the view from both signal boxes (and much of the remainder of the station) was seriously hindered.

(R.C.Riley Coll.)

Kings Cross had been built at a cost of £123,000 before 'additions in the shape of small suburban stations' took place. Fashion in taste cast it in different light over the years; at times its styling seemed at best irrelevant but now it is applauded, and stoutly defended. It is indeed worth recalling that in the 1950s and parts of the 1960s almost anything 'Victorian' was routinely excoriated; 'Gothic', as typified by St. Pancras was mocked and its removal presented almost as a public service. In 1932, however, the station had been celebrated as an octogenarian by the LNER; Cubitt's frontage and the great train sheds were 'thought a great deal of .. it wore a magnificent appearance and presented an extraordinary vista'. Some of the original shareholders however would not have been impressed by this and were not enamoured at the time of its building. There were complaints of the extravagance involved: 'To their criticisms Edmund Denison, famous chairman of the old Great Northern, characteristically replied, 'I am authorised to state that it is the cheapest building for what it contains and will contain, that can be pointed out in London; I am told — I am not the architect and I do not estimate it — that it will not have cost more than £123,500. If that is the case, I have no difficulty at all in saying that it is a very cheap station. Bear in mind, however, that we paid by arbitration and award, I think, about £65,000 for the two old buildings that stood there, and then we had to excavate the ground before the station was erected; so I do not pretend to say that the whole cost is only about £123,000....' Kings Cross, befitting a great station, was long a place of milestones in the history of British railways; in 1879 the first railway dining car left the station, provided with foodstuffs from the Kings Cross cellars. In 1888 it was the starting point for the expresses of the East Coast companies in their race against those of the West Coast to Edinburgh, and 1894 saw the first British track circuit ... 'and the longest railway race in these islands took place in 1895 ... before a truce was patched, King's Cross witnessed the departure of an express which cut down the original timing to Aberdeen of 11 hours 35 minutes to no less than 8 hours 40 minutes — a throughout speed of over 60 mph despite the fact that engines were changed at six points en route. In 1921 the first restaurant car in the world to be fitted with an electric kitchen [a worthy development, no doubt, but hardly ranking foremost in the pantheon of transport achievement] left King's Cross on a Leeds express; the year 1927 saw a new world's record in non-stop train running set up by the 9.50 a.m. from King's Cross which covered the 268½ miles non-stop to Newcastle; in May 1928, this record was broken by the 'Flying Scotsman' which from then until the present day (during the summer months) makes a world's record non-stop run between King's Cross and Edinburgh — a distance of 392½ miles...' Above is Platform 10, the old No.1 Departure, and the high Kings Cross vaults at their best. Two trains, at least in later days, are unusual. The bridge proclaiming 'Owbridge's Lung Tonic' was put up in 1893 along with the new platforms (to become 5 and 6) either side of the central dividing wall. The Lung Tonic was peculiarly apt, for smoke wreathed and curled itself across the bridge, a strange place to be as the hollow, crashing groan of engines rolled through the station and reverberated from the great roofs. This was the side of the original offices, which were thought to sufficiently compensate the expansionary tendencies of the laminated timber girders. They acted as 'stretched bows' and were replaced on the east arrival side, where there was no compensating office structure, in 1870 'at a cost of £13,000.' The east departure side was similarly dealt with in 1886/7 and Johns relates how a travelling wooden stage on wheels was used for the work. It was put into store, he recounts, after the work of the 1860s and the numbered parts reassembled for the 1880s.

(Camden Libraries, National Railway Museum)

Yard' as well as ... 'the Viaduct in the Goods Yard, with Skew Bridge', the lot costed at £5112.18s.9d.

Colonel Yolland for the Board of Trade inspected the new 'Gas Works', or 'Maiden Lane' Tunnel on 20th February and reported on 27th. He described the ballast as *burnt clay, gravel and coarse sand .... constructed in London clay. This railway has been made longer than intended ....* [presumably referring to the new work to serve as rebuilt York Road] *...and connections are not complete. Signals are also incomplete, and improvements at the York Road station are in hand. These two new lines are intended for the fast and slow up traffic to Kings Cross and the Co. desire permission to make use of one of them, adjacent to York Road station, before the works are complete, to give facilities to alter the arrangement of lines in the station yard. The permanent way in a portion of the tunnel is laid too high, there not being sufficient clearance ....* The inspector sanctioned use of the line to 'further expedite the work' but the problem of clearance had, he warned, to be attended 'at once'. Matters proceeded more or less without hitch after this and the second Gas Works bore 'was taken into use on Monday, March 4th 1878', a few days after Yolland's Board of Trade Report.

The doubling of capacity afforded by the new works meant a breathing space only; for years developments at Kings Cross had only stumbled a step or two ahead of an operating quagmire. The great part of the main line departures, for instance, still used only the one original western platform, the latter day No.10, but named for many years, with some logic, 'No.1 Departure'. Johns quotes Acworth in *The Railways of England: The Kings Cross porters despatch human beings, and the Finsbury Park people collect tickets, faster than on any line I know.*

Work was soon in hand to increase line capacity even further and as before the Copenhagen Tunnel had to be enlarged first. A third double line bore was authorised by a Great Northern Railway Act of 1882 for 'Widening at Islington' and 'Contract No.1' was accepted and signed by Mr Henry Lovatt of Wolverhampton, at £90,048.10s.4d, amended the next day to £90,298.10s.4d. This tunnel was the worst of the three in terms of construction; it had to be driven to the west of the original, was shallow in comparison to its predecessors and 'trade and industrie' had huddled about 'The Caley' (the Caledonian Road) above, variously noxious and benign. The third Copenhagen Tunnel consisted of *a railway commencing at four furlongs two and a half chains by a junction with the Company's Main Line at or near the south face of the bridge carrying the North London Railway over that line and terminating at one mile nine chains, 'GN mileage', by a junction with the said Main Line about three chains north of the north-east of the bridge carrying the Caledonian Road over the said Main Line.* These were the years when London, now almost entirely deindustrialised, was possibly the manufacturing and processing centre of *The World*; the tunnel was to run under Blundell Street, Brewery Road, Market Road and the Caledonian Road and the factories to be underpinned read like a cavalcade of industrial ghosts: 'Messrs Gorridge & Co. Varnish Works, Messrs Crosse & Blackwell's Vinegar Brewery, Mr Kennedy's Albumen Works and Messrs Knight & Sons, Melters.' The bore was to be lined in 'good sound stock bricks', with recesses for p.w. staff ('sanctuaries') on 'each side 50ft apart'. The existing cattle pens at Holloway were to be 'removed and replaced'. This third Copenhagen bore came into use in June 1886 and from 1890 steps were taken to replicate it with a third Gas Works Tunnel. Close to the surface and the Kings Cross goods yard above, it made for some tricky subterranean work

and it opened in the summer of 1892. The Great Northern had written to the Board of Trade on 6th May asking for the signalling works in connection with the new tunnel to be inspected; together with the 'first instalment of signalling of same from the West Box', it would be ready for use '10 days from 6th instant'.

Major Marindin inspected on 7th June and found the interlocking incorrect (few companies ever got it right straight off) and was obviously unhappy about the second hand signal frame the thrifty GN had harnessed for the task. The company wrote again on 20th July, answering that 'good progress has been made with the work of altering the signalling ... it will be ready for reinspection on 7th August.' The Board of Trade was still less than keen and requested a new frame in the West Box, a demand eventually complied with the following year ... 'The new frame was inspected on 20th April 1893 ... there are 98 working levers and 42 spare levers'.

This was just as well, for only in that year* (astonishingly, for the station had been working more than 40 years) was an additional main line departure platform provided. Late in 1893, in December, a proper double-faced platform was built, in the middle of the station, latterly numbered 5 and 6 but then termed No.5 Arrival and (on the west side) No.2 Departure.

There was now a long pause in such upheavals at Kings Cross, until LNER days, though from the early 1890s a number of less obvious alterations took place. The suburban side, tucked out of the way on the west side, was soon tackled; the loco yard continued its slow journey westwards. The island platform followed it to give an extra road; three tracks, each enjoying a platform face, were now available, in place of the previous two tracks/three platform faces. The curving line off the Metropolitan was rendered somewhat less formidable and a separate platform made available on its west side. Largely cut off from view, by the waiting rooms and a wall, this became Platform A, latterly that is, No.16 and 17, and remained the most westerly at Kings Cross. The building upheavals did little to dispel the pokey nature of 'the suburban side' and it remained a place of sudden turns and narrow walkways, but all was made more or less good, and opened for traffic, by April 1895.

Reading east to west from the platform alongside the west wall (known from 1924 as No.11) to the new line A, the platforms were titled E,D,C(loco yard in between),B, and A. The whole lot was further altered in 1924, with removal of the loco yard (to its familiar site by the Gas Works Tunnel) and the insinuation of a new double platform − but see later.

The station seems to have operated now with three up and three down lines; two down in the third, westernmost Gasworks Tunnel, two up through the second, easterly bore and a down and up line in the original, now the middle, tunnel. This last, original line served as 'up carriage line', for light engines, empty stock and as a shunting spur. In 1898 further alterations were made 'for the purpose of providing additional facilities for getting empty carriage trains into Kings Cross'. For this 'an existing shunting neck' (apparently 'South London Siding') at Belle Isle was converted to a running line 'entered by a facing connection on the up main line opposite Belle Isle signal box. In consequence a new down box was built, 'Belle Isle Down', to give three boxes in the short stretch between Copenhagen and Gas Works Tunnels, from

Johns notes the working timetable for July 1st 1893, a scheduled daily total of 539 trains, 274 down and 265 up. This included 77 down and 79 up goods working through the Metropolitan tunnels and no less than 98 passenger trains each way over the 'Met'.

the south: 'Copenhagen Box', 'Belle Isle Up Box' and now 'Belle Isle Down Box'. This new line, the 'up carriage', was the only one with connection to all platforms, as Johns relates and from January 1922 it was 'renamed the up relief and resignalled to permit passenger train working, whilst retaining its usefulness for other types of movement'. With this the strict division of the station into arrival and departure sides was ended, though the effects on platform numbering, and consequent passenger confusion and ire continued for many years.

LNER Efforts

Two new platforms were put in at the suburban station on the site of the loco yard, as mentioned earlier, Nos. 14 and 15 with umbrella roof. Since 1906 the Great Northern had been promoting the delights of its rural catchment and Jackson has already noted some of the startling descriptions – 'Bracing Barnet' and among others, and particularly bizarre, 'Picturesque Finchley'. These were *The Northern Heights* writ large; 'Londons Healthiest and most Accessible Suburbs' and GN services made it possible to combine 'The Pleasures of the Country with the Privileges of Town'. The GN publicity booklet was entitled somewhat uncompromisingly *Where to Live* and though by the 1930s the LNER was glad to cast off much of the traffic to the Piccadilly and Northern lines, the new suburban platforms were much needed. *Traffic Improvements at Kings Cross*, an official LNER Report on engineering progress at the terminus, appeared anonymously (though clearly provided by the LNER) in *The Railway Magazine* of 1924 and described the problems. Kings Cross had begun to labour under the strict division between departures and arrivals and for many years 'quite as many' suburban trains ('on a large and growing scale') had originated or arrived at the main line station as were using the up and down Metropolitan connections. Indeed: *For a considerable time ... it has been the practice during the busy periods to schedule many of the down suburban trains from Moorgate Street to pass the platform provided for them on the steep incline from the Metropolitan Railway,* [the Hotel Curve] *suburban traffic from the main line station itself being largely provided for by separate trains.*

These latter trains of course had to shunt across the station after their arrival to gain the departure platform. Some sophistry was needed to overcome the obvious drawbacks of all this and the key was the conversion of the 'up carriage' into a standard running line, the 'up relief'. Up trains could thereby run directly into all the platforms on the departure side. 'No point alterations' were involved but there was extensive resignalling, 'and in connection therewith the principles of

The contrast, St Pancras/Kings Cross, was perhaps the most dramatic in the capital and has remained one of the most striking. In the 1950s and 1960s both were derided, one as 'Gothic out of control' and the other well, out of control. With the fate of Euston just up the road, it is perhaps a small miracle that both of these brilliant buildings, juxtaposed by chance, remain with us. For years the Great Northern felt itself in the shade, and the exuberance of St Pancras, it was considered, made The Cross *a dull place.*

three-position and upper-quadrant signalling have been adapted to the circumstances of the situation in a manner which introduces several interesting and novel features.'

The LNER, principally through Mr. Brown CBE, the Chief Engineer, provided an exhaustive description of the new signalling which makes for recommended reading. Its crucial feature was that up trains could now directly enter the surburban side and although the station approach remained 'very complicated' (an understatement) and certain movements had a profound blocking effect (principally those outwards from 1 to 5 which halted all inward movements) things were nevertheless much improved. There were now eleven roads in the main station and the old separate designation 1-5 for arrivals (all of which served platforms) and 1-2 for departures (these served platforms with 4 sidings in between) was abandoned. All lines (not platforms, note) were now renumbered from the original No.1. Thus 1-5 remained the same, No. 2 departure became No.6 and the ancient No.1 departure, No.10. This slightly perverse sequence (maintaining a long history of the same) gave 1-6, 10 in the main station, allowing for the removal of one of the four sidings on the old departure side to be taken out and a long narrow platform inserted, numbered 7 and 8 in September 1926. No. 9 *siding* was absorbed when Platform 7/8 was doubled in width in 1938. In the meantime in 1934 the LNER had abolished the stepped platform 3, for the series to run, by the end of the 'thirties .. 1&2, 4-8, 10. The local platforms beyond the west wall were numbered 11-17 in the scheme, incorporating the new umbrella roofed 14 and 15.

It still made little obvious sense, and total confusion time — say five minutes for every new or occasional passenger — could possibly add up to centuries.

The York Road station. It remained a strange place, cobbled to the last and treacherous in winter, and never shook off a certain hangdog air. It only came alive of course in the morning rush; the great part of those alighting were obliged to trudge southwards to their work, or to the Underground, a walk down York Way by the blank windswept eastern side of the station. More interestingly, a course could be plotted (particularly popular in the wet) along Platform 1, picking one's way through trollies, parcels and mail bags.
(G. Dunsbury Coll.)

Earlier times in the suburban ('the local') station where wooden boards lent an odd muffling to the usual hubbub. This and the view below should be 1934; the 11.50am was 'The Scarborough Flier' and the four hours ten minutes fixes it in that year.

(National Railway Museum)

Both this photograph and the one above depict Nos. 11 and 12 platform ends. To walk in here was to enter something of a different world from the main part of the station – it was to experience suddenly, by comparison, a sort of country, almost provincial air. On the right is a chocolate machine (upright) and that now long–vanished phenomenon, the name printing machine, in which the customer chose an alloy label, letter by letter.

(National Railway Museum)

The East Box in May 1931. Both the Kings Cross boxes were squat affairs, crude of aspect and ancient in years. They obviously replaced some original, primitive provision, and reflected the absolute division at the terminus between up and down working.

(National Railway Museum)

A Signal Event

The LNER Board heard of the antiquated signalling at the terminus on 22nd January 1930....

The signalling at the Kings Cross Passenger Station which is manually operated — is controlled from two signal boxes known as 'Kings Cross East' and 'Kings Cross West'. The number of working levers in the East box is 76 and the West box 137 — a total of 213.

The existing plant is worn out; it requires constant attention and repair, and is becoming difficult to maintain in a safe and satisfactory condition. The signalboxes also require renewal. With the present system of manual working, it is not considered practicable to combine the two boxes in one, partly because it would be difficult to find a site large enough to accommodate a box of the requisite dimensions, and partly on account of the dislocation and risk which would result consequent on new runs of rodding and wires having to be put in places where there is inadequate room for the purpose, seeing that they would have to be installed, as far as possible, before the existing runs are interfered with.

It is therefore proposed to install power working on an all-electric system, with colour lighting. This would enable the working to be concentrated in one box, for which there would be no difficulty in finding a site on account of the requisite dimensions being much smaller: Estimated cost...£46,200.

The power system would enable the present operating staff of 13 men and 4 boys spread over 3 shifts, to be replaced by 8 men and 3 boys, while the existing maintenance staff of 12 could be reduced to 10. This amounts to a decrease in annual costs of £1,114....

These proposals were recommended by the Chief General Manager, Ralph Wedgwood, who returned to the issue, in mournful mood, on 25th October 1932: *The Directors will have seen reference in the press to the dislocation at Kings Cross at the commencement of this month, consequent upon alterations in signalling at that place and it is thought they would like to have before them a report of the matter.*

The scheme is that sanctioned by Traffic Committee Minute 4512 of 30th January 1930 at an estimated cost of £46,200 which, briefly, provides for the replacement of the two mechanical signalboxes known as the East and West boxes respectively by one central 'all-electric' box. The Directors authorised the placing of the contract with Messrs. Siemens & General Electric Railway Signal Co. at a cost of £34,901.0s.10d. on 24th July 1930.

A programme was drawn up for the changeover to be effected in three stages, as under:

First Stage. Signals at Belle Isle — North end of Gas Works Tunnels, 19th June 1932.

Second Stage. All West Box working. 2nd October 1932.

Third Stage (final). East Box working. 30th October 1932.

The First Stage was carried out to programme and no hitch occurred. The Second Stage was commenced at 1 o'clock on the morning of Sunday October 2nd and the schedule of operations provided that all points and signals should be capable of being worked from the new box by 6pm, the period from 6pm on Sunday to 6am on Monday 3rd — during which it was arranged we should have possession of the west side of the yard — being utilised in testing all signal circuits and controls. Trouble began however with the first pairs of double ended points which were coupled up as it was found that when being operated one of the motors, after the movement appeared to have been completed, was rotating for a short period in the reverse direction, sufficient to cause a movement of the point

detectors and break down the detection contacts. The breaking down of these contacts prevented the running signals from being operated, thus causing delay to traffic operations, hand signalling being resorted to. Investigations showed that this was brought about by the fact that the two motors had been connected up in parallel with only two wires from the cabin to the first pair of points and as their movements did not exactly terminate at the same moment, current from the motor which had not quite completed its stroke passed through the field coils of the other one causing the short reverse movement mentioned above. Each motor should have been operated by an independent pair of wires and double contacts, involving running four wires from the box, but for reasons of their own the contractors had altered this and utilised one pair of wires only, as previously stated. As a temporary measure the motors have been 'cascaded', by which, one motor has to complete its movement before the other begins to operate, thereby preventing the reverse action which gave rise to the trouble. This has the effect of slowing up the combined movement where double ended points are concerned and the question of installing separate pairs of wires from the cabin to each motor of double ended pairs of points is in hand with the contractors.

Owing to the time occupied in altering temporarily the wiring to the more important of these points it was not until 4.30am on Monday that the last of them which it was necessary to couple up to the box, were completed, and even then, those leading into the loco yard had to be left uncoupled, and operated by hand signalling and clamps. By the morning of Tuesday 4th the last of this 'cascading' was done, thereby removing this trouble. The fault here rests with the contractors, who should not have adopted the system of wiring they did.

Another difficulty which was experienced in the initial stages were those from the rather fine setting in the first instance of the detectors. This was done in the interests of safety and is not a matter in which we can find fault with the contractors but is incidental to the bringing into operation of such works as these. By slightly coarsening the detection, the vibratory action of the trains on the detection contacts was counteracted, though, of course, the points which fitted up quite closely to their stock rails were not affected. The necessary adjustments in this case were completed by the evening of Tuesday 4th.

Inside the East Box. A very extensive programme of resignalling and interlocking took place on the southern part of the Great Northern in the 1870s and 1880s, though the East Box was not concerned in a substantial scheme at Kings Cross, completed in 1881. It always had fewer levers than the West Box — less than 50 in the 1880s and 76 by 1930.

(National Railway Museum)

The terminus in relatively quiescent mood, engines and stock having rattled out of sight. Battle Bridge Road and Congreve Street were low and squat and together with the restriction and poor visibility imposed by the tunnels and station layout made for unpleasant awkwardness in the working of the terminus. Battle Bridge in particular 'was a great hindrance to train movements; it obstructed the view and caused much smoke and steam to collect, and its removal had been contemplated for a number of years' (Kings Cross Then and Now, W.J. Reynolds, Railway World, 1952). The crunch came with the need for the new loco yard; the GN purchased 5¾ acres from the adjacent Gas Light and Coke Co. and powers were obtained for the removal of Battle Bridge Road together with Congreve Street bridge − 'called so by the railway but in our recollection extending over nearly 40 years, this entrance to the Gas Works, the sole use of the bridge, has never been known by a name.' Another roadway had to be substituted, between York Road and Pancras Road; named with something less than panache, 'Goods Way', it ran over the top of the Gas Works Tunnels adjacent to the Regents Canal. The resignalling project, as Wedgwood reports, was sanctioned on 30th January 1930 and the contract let to Siemens on 24th July the same year. Various preliminary works however determined that it should not get under way for some two years, the First Stage to be completed in June 1932 and the ill-fated Second and Third Stages due for completion in the autumn. The new signal box is slowly appearing behind the squat West Box in the centre of this view. Much of the station's appearance and its mode of operation in 1931 derived from the early LNER work of the 1920s; Kings Cross had always been an inordinately complicated place and the new upper quadrants for instance (one is in the left foreground − 97 and 98 − and the other beyond − 93 and 99) represented a way of overcoming the permissive nature of much of the movement. With empty carriages and light engines, nevertheless, 'you went everywhere at caution' … All movements thus provided for, including those of trains or engines on the up carriage line as far as the disc signal within the tunnel were therefore, of a shunting character. Owing to the complications, and the large number of points and connections crowded into small space, it was virtually impossible to give complete indications of all movements, and discs controlling movement from stage to stage had to suffice. This arrangement has worked well for many years, but obviously trains conveying passengers could not be worked into the station by this route; hence the need for alterations and the new equipment … The new signals satisfied the rules as they applied to passenger running and were also equipped with miniature arms which control the movements of empty trains and engines, as previously provided for, with the further improvement that, by using route indicating appliances, drivers are now given full information as to where they are proceeding, whether with passenger trains or under shunting conditions. The miniature arms here are 97 and 99, the main signals 98 and 93. 101 at the north end of Gas Works Tunnel was close to Belle Isle Down cabin but was controlled from Kings Cross West Box. It in turn was an upper quadrant ('an innovation for the GN') and its 45° and 90° indications repeated one or other of the new stop signals above, 97/98 and 93/99. These controlled further movement into the terminus. The two main arms, 97 and 99 indicated restricted movement and the indicators, manufactured by Siemens, were of the roller blind type, 'bearing the necessary numerals or letters' to denote the platforms to which the signals were leading. The roller wound on until the appropriate place, at which it stopped, a lamp to illuminate it both sides then coming on automatically. The new engine yard on the right was ever crowded and noisy, even in diesel days and the constant 'shunt duties' (not 'pilots' at Kings Cross) and freights to and from the Metropolitan added to the general clamour. The third line from the left is the familiar 'Northern Spur', a siding or 'lye' where the shunt duties frequently 'laid over'. A van stands beyond on the 'Centre Spur', where the line plunges into the Met. The bufferstops of the Centre Spur mark almost the precise position of the most northerly of the two road bridges crossing the station yard − the so called Congreve Street.

(National Railway Museum)

The most serious trouble however was the false indication given by the point detector relays in the signalbox, which began to show itself on Tuesday. This was found to be due to the fact that in some cases when the point lever was operated the relay contacts swung right over to the reverse instead of into the neutral position and at times held in that position even though the points themselves were normal. The effect of this when it occurred was not only to give wrong indication to the signalman but would have enabled him to obtain conflicting movements. The danger of allowing such a condition to continue is self evident and the steps to remedy it were taken without delay. The whole of these point detector relays so far as the new signalling has been brought into use have been replaced by those of the Westinghouse type, the work being done on the weekends of the 8th/9th and 15th/16th instant, these being the only periods on which possession of the track could be obtained for times necessary for the changeover to be made.

It will be appreciated that the defects which made themselves felt on the morning of 3rd October, caused a dislocation of traffic. Great difficulty was experienced in dealing with the 'rush hour' suburban trains and this reacted on the mainline trains, which suffered heavy delay both outward and inward. Every effort was made by the traffic department to mitigate inconvenience. Serious delay to main line trains was practically confined to the Monday, October 3rd, normal working being virtually restored on Tuesday October 4th. In an attempt to relieve the situation with regard to suburban working, the fullest possible use was made of the Moorgate lines, whilst a number of trains due to run to and from the terminal station were terminated at Finsbury Park and the public advised to use the Underground to and from Finsbury Park and Kings Cross. In spite of this, however, very numerous delays took place and it was not found possible to run the full suburban service until Monday 24th October.

It has been deemed advisable to defer the carrying out of the Third Stage of the changeover until all the difficulties which arose on the Second Stage have been satisfactorily dealt with. The question of the liability of the contractors has been fully considered by Mr Brown, whose report thereon will be submitted with this memo to the Works Committee.....Brown's subsequent experiences are charted in the accompanying captions.

The dismal West Box in May 1931. It had 90 levers in 1881 when it controlled 'all outgoing signals'. Its relation to the new box is obvious.

(National Railway Musueum)

Inside the West Box ('to be demolished') on 27th May 1931, a clattering, noisy place, of much rattling and shaking as levers crashed in its elderly frame and engines and trains rumbled by.

(National Railway Museum)

'New electric signal box', 11th November 1932. It had been built by E.R. Hipperson & Sons, awarded the contract on 24th January 1931, at £1811.0s.0d. and it was presumably infinitely more comfortable than either of its predecessors. Its operation was quieter and it stood markedly above the trains; it even boasted 'hot water heating', supplied by Dilworth & Carr for £133. In any memory of Kings Cross in steam days this huge box plays a great part, though its internal operation remained a deep mystery.

(National Railway Museum)

The Kings Cross diagram; it would be nice to think that some fragments of this box survive, unsuspected, in some cherished collection today.

(National Railway Museum)

View over the main line departure platforms on 31st March 1933. Kings Cross had been entirely transformed by this time; the Siemens scheme despite the initial setbacks was operating, much of 'the gubbins' carried in the distinctive 'access gallery'. The two bridges straddling the yard had long gone, to be replaced by 'Goods Way' and even the upper quadrants so acclaimed in 1924 had gone. The project had been a prestige one from the beginning and attracted fierce competition; two tenders had been received for electric pneumatic systems and four on the 'all electric' principle. Charles Brown the LNER Engineer was inclined to the latter and Siemens provided the best quote ... 'as to which system should be adopted, the all electric type is the more modern one and I should prefer to see it installed', Brown wrote to the Works Committee (as Wedgwood said he would; see text, and the LNER travails with Siemens) on 17th June 1932 ... the order to commence work was given to Siemens on 9th October 1930, and should have been completed by 10th October 1931, under penalty of £100 [underlined in red in the original] per week for every week or part of a week during which the work remains incomplete. Difficulties in connection with the execution of the work have been much greater than anticipated ... it was hoped that matters would be sufficiently far advanced to enable the working controlled from the old West Box to be transferred to the new box and brought into operation for the commencement of the summer traffic on 18th July next, the East Box being dealt with later. While the work, so far as affecting the West Box will be complete by that date there will be insufficient time to enable a thorough test to be made ... Despite difficulties, I consider the contractors could have shown more foresight ... a modified penalty will be due ... (i.e.) the cost of keeping the old box open — a special record is being kept of this cost. Contract extended from 10th October 1931 to mid-June 1932 ... with one month additional to permit of the new electric apparatus being thoroughly tested out before the summer traffic is, I consider, reasonable in the circumstances and should have been more than sufficient for the purpose.

(National Railway Museum)

A3 No.2505 Cameronian *on time with* The Silver Jubilee. *Such an engine on this train was out of the ordinary and the clock reveals the unstreamlined Pacific to be perfectly competent on the job. Did any of its passengers view it with dismay, disappointed at an 'ordinary' green one instead of a much-vaunted Silver Bullet ...?*

(A.B.Collins Coll.)

Grounded partly at least in a highly efficient publicity machine, the 'Kings Cross departure' became something of an institution in railway lore. This seems to be a scene from the 1920s, before 1928, for there are no headboards, and the trains are therefore not non–stop. In its quest for as much publicity as it could milk from the undoubtedly prestigious routes to Yorkshire and Scotland, the LNER had no better ally than the Gresley Pacifics. Always (well nearly always) in smart condition, the Pacifics, clothed in their grass green livery, provided an impressive and glamorous image in an otherwise grime laden environment. Teak varnished coaches completed an elegant ensemble that caught the atmosphere of the day.

(Brian Hilton Coll.)

If there was a typical Kings Cross locomotive it was probably the 0-6-2T, and though 2662 (seen in 1931) is an N2, N1s would probably have a greater claim to be the representative Kings Cross type. A3s or A4s, even Brush Type 2s (Class 31s) or Deltics would also have a claim. Ponderous and strangely-proportioned their thudding progress and black livery, and the outriding 'handle bar' condenser pipes characterised the cavernous Kings Cross. The condensers provided for an eerie effect in the tunnels, the tank filler lid lifting rhythmically with puffs of steam but they were almost never put to use, at least post-Second World War. For the Metropolitan lines, trip gear was in use and this was strictly enforced, the signalmen under instructions to 'trip out' the night goods as a test.

(Gordon Coltas)

The new loco yard, 9th June 1931. It was generally known simply as 'the passenger, or bottom, loco' and was one of the earliest sites for LNER mechanised coal apparatus. It was a particular joy that at Kings Cross the engine yard was largely visible from the platforms nearby, though something particularly interesting always seemed to lurk just out of sight, reluctant to come forth. This was a feature which continued unabated into diesel days; all sorts used it, the N2s on a two shift system were brought in there for an hour or so to clean fires and generally 'square up' or a Grantham loco might come in for servicing while the visiting natives took their tea and grub. The junior Kings Cross men frequently relieved crews at the platform, bringing engines back to the passenger loco, but Royal Sovereign, marking time on Cambridge trains, was an exception; no one was allowed on the 'Royal.' Although there was no LNER shed proper at this location, its servicing facilities were the 'bottom' opposite of 'Top' shed, and the justification for the latter's name. The 'Top' did not mean it took pride of place amongst GN sheds, something that New England, Grantham, and Doncaster would have fiercely contested. The best that 34A could have claimed would be primus inter pares.

(Thompson Society)

No. 2001 Cock o'the North *was sent new in 1934 to Kings Cross for trials. Much has been written about this small but famous class of locomotive but it is interesting to note that 2001 was the first engine to thrill us with the Gresley three–cylinder Kylchap sound, as well as the famous chime whistle – still enjoyable today through the preserved A4s and the unlikely agency of that marvellous reincarnation* Duke of Gloucester.

(A.B.Collins Coll.)

Atlantic (the 'M2' denotes 'Down Main Line No.2') No. 4449 picking its way about the station yard. Such engines dominated Kings Cross before the Pacific era and indeed continued on many important trains long after. An article in Railway World *of 1954 by the late Reginald H. Coe ('Around the London Termini 40 years ago') praised the remarkable powers of these engines. One was held to have brought in a 'Scotch Express' of no less than twenty two eight wheel vehicles and in a precursor of many subsequent laments, their post First World War condition was held to be 'indeed a saddening sight.'*

(A.B.Collins Coll.)

GREAT NORTHERN SIGNALLING PLAN

Submitted to the Board of Trade in 1898; uniquely interesting, it shows the alterations carried out "for the purpose of providing additional facilities for getting empty carriage trains into Kings Cross, for which purpose an existing shunting neck has been converted into a running line, which is entered by a facing connection on the up main line opposite Belle Isle signal box. In consequence of this a new signal box has been built at Belle Isle and certain signals which led out onto the shunting neck at Kings Cross have been removed." The plan is of particular value for it shows both bridges crossing the station yard and highlights the cramped and awkward nature of working The Cross. Of the three engine spurs only the "Northern" is labelled but the other two, "Central" and "Southern" can be made out clearly, one either side of the East Box.

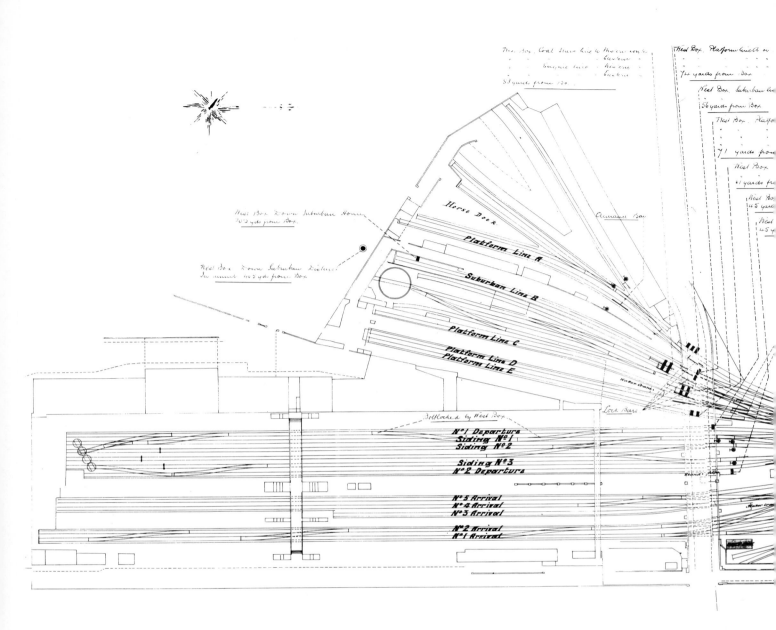

The Kings Cross *norf* London townscape in 1936, which among other things reveals the Great Northern Hotel to be a third jewel, now of course proposed for demolition – for a description see later. The cluttered buildings before the station screen were probably at their most heterogeneous, with a little bit of 1930s art deco creeping in. Newly erected is perhaps the oddest building to grace the scene, the Laings Show House, where passing commuters (actually a post War term, unheard-of in the 1930s) were urged to seek the country delights. 'Pretty villages and Hertfordshire' and 'Country homes in Bedfordshire and Cambridgeshire' had been advertised for some thirty years. The lower middle class flight from Islington villas continued and the 1930s successor became the Laings detached and semi detached, brick built, tile roofed and curved steel windows. The call, 'Exchange fog for sunshine' reflected the winter smog of the capital.

(Copenhagen Friends)

Kings Cross East Box		Kings Cross West Box		Belle Isle Down Box		Belle Isle Up Box	
Locking Frame		Locking Frame		Locking Frame		Locking Frame	
Signals	26	Signals	41	Signals	12	Signals	23
Ground discs	17	Ground discs	17	Points	3	Points	5
Points	16	Points	32	Lock Bars	2	Lock Bars	5
Bolt Locks	2	Bolt Locks	1	Clearance Bars	5	Clearance Bars	3
Lock Bars	14	Lock Bars	29		22	Releasing	1
Clearance Bars	2	Clearance Bars	2	Spare	3		37
Gong	1	Gong	1		25	Spare	3
Releasing	1	Bells	2				40
	79		125				
Spare	21	Spare	15				
	100		140				

GRADIENT DIAGRAM.

LEVEL — 1 IN 105 — 1 IN 110

0   ¼   ½   ¾   1   1¼ MILES

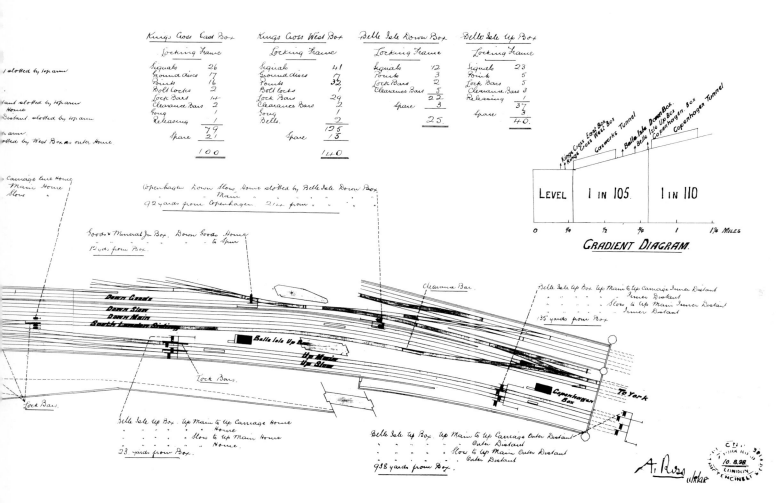

Left side notes:
- ...slotted by top arm
- ...tant slotted by top arm Home
- ...Distant slotted by top arm
- ...arm
- ...tted by West Box as outer Home
- ...Carriage line Home Main Home Slow
- Lock Bars.
- Lock Bars.

Centre notes:
- Goods & Mineral Jn Box, Down Goods Home to Spur 12 yds from Box.
- Copenhagen Down Slow Home slotted by Belle Isle Down Box Main 92 yards from Copenhagen 21¼ from "
- Belle Isle Up Box. Up Main to Up Carriage Home Home " Slow to Up Main Home " Home 23 yards from Box.
- Belle Isle Up Box. Up Main to Up Carriage Outer Distant Outer Distant " Slow to Up Main Outer Distant Outer Distant 938 yards from Box.

Track labels:
- Down Goods
- Down Slow
- Down Main
- Branch Lanesboro Sidings
- Belle Isle Up Box
- Up Main
- Up Slow
- Lock Bars.
- Clearance Bar.
- Copenhagen Box
- To York

Right side notes:
- Belle Isle Up Box Up Main to Up Carriage Inner Distant " Inner Distant " Slow to Up Main Inner Distant Inner Distant 135 yards from Box

Gradient diagram top labels:
Kings Cross East Box, Kings Cross West Box, Gasworks Tunnel, Belle Isle Down Box, Belle Isle Up Box, Copenhagen Box, Copenhagen Tunnel

A. Ross Engineer

G.N.R. Kings Cross to Belle Isle

Plan shewing Signals

Scale 50 Feet

9767

West Box. Western route to Down Slow
Main No 2
Eastern
No 1 Departure to Down Main No 2
Sidings No 1. 2 or 3 &
1. 2. 3. Northern Spur
No 2 Departure to Down Main No 2
Northern Spur.

West Box. Set back Down Slow
50 yds from West Box

West Box. Set back Down Main No 1
Up Carriage to coal stage
Engine line, platform lines C. D. & E.
or No 1 Departure
57 yds from Box

West Box. Catch to Down Main No 1
142 yds from Box

West Box. Set back Down Main No 2
190 yds from Box

Belle Isle Down Box. Down Slow to Down Goods Distant
Slotted by West Box as down Slow Advance on one lever.
618 yards from Belle Isle Down Box. 109 yards from West Box.

Belle Isle Down Box. Down Main No 2 Distant
slotted by West Box as Advance.
617 yards from Belle Isle Down Box. 110 yards from West Box.

Belle Isle Down Box. Down Main No 1 to Down Goods Distant
Distant
slotted by West Box as Down Advance on one lever
617 yds from Belle Isle Down Box & 110 yds from West Box.

West Box Up Carriage Inner Home
Lamp in Tunnel 142 yards from Box.

West Box. Set back Down Slow, Bell
180 yds from Box.

West Box. Set back Down Main No 2, Gong
172 yards from Box.

West Box. Set back Down Main No 1, Bell
279 yards from Box.

Mocking safety switch

Lock Bars.
Lock Bars
Lock Bars
Lock Bars.

Down Slow
Down Main No 2
Down Main No 1
Northern Spur
Up Main
Up Slow
platform
Road

Down Slow
Down Main No 2
Down Main No 1
Up Carriage

Belle Isle Down Box

Clearance Bars
Clearance Bars

East Box. Up Main No 5 Arrival Distant slotted by Belle Isle Up Box
3
1
2
706 yards from East Box. 220 yds from Belle Isle Up Box.

East Box. arrival lines to Down lines stop signals
slotted by West Box on one lever.

Belle Isle Up Box. South London Siding
95 yards from Box.

2566 and 2750 hitched together in 1930. This was a favourite device at The Cross, linking engines in twos and threes to ease the movement difficulties in and out of the terminus.

*Silver Link **stirring interest. Note the platform numbering, an illustration of the layout idiosyncrasies enjoyed at The Cross. Such eccentricities persisted until electrification***

Drivers in the 1930s were less than famous for their sartorial elegance! This stalwart, under a goodly covering of Blidworth coal dust, poses for the publicity shot, seeming to explain an indelicate part of the anatomy of the silver fox adornment ... The gentleman in the top hat is the station master, the date December 19th 1935

(A. B. Collins Coll.)

Condenser J52 No. 3922 awaits entry into the Metropolitan tunnel at York Road. Known as 'starvers' at Hornsey, these little engines were capable of hauling trains of up to 20 loaded coal wagons, to such exotic destinations as Battersea, Herne Hill, Bricklayers Arms and New Cross Gate. The collection of buildings to the rear of the picture accommodated various organisations, such as the British Legion and the Westinghouse Brake & Saxby Signal Co.

(A.B. Collins Coll.)

A Direct Hit

The Second World War brought appalling conditions of toil, hardship and fear to Kings Cross, punctuated and relieved by valour and a grim good humour. As the dread of the first days faded there came months of almost comic disruption and overcrowding. Inconvenience and delay were the worst experiences and even the grim harvest of Dunkirk made for traffic difficulties more then anything else. When the bombs came a new War began.

As the campaign hardened bomb damage across the great empire that was then the LNER grew and by 7th September 1940 had been costed at £29,650 in the Southern Area, £9,150 in the North Eastern Area, £2,100 in Scotland and £2,100 at the various docks. After the 7th attacks were increasingly concentrated on the Southern Area. Kings Cross engine shed and the potato market were hit, four engines were damaged in Peterborough engine yard, killing an engineman and injuring 10 others and in January Colchester and Liverpool Street were attacked. Ipswich station was machine gunned, killing a

guard and at Lowestoft 8 LNER men and a customs officer were killed and 34 railwaymen were injured. On the night of Saturday 10th/11th May 1941 Kings Cross, Liverpool Street and Marylebone were all hit, with the Cross the worst:

A high explosive bomb struck part of the main station building, the western block facing No. 10 platform and considerable damage occurred. There were unfortunately 9 fatalities, 4 of the company's men and 5 soldiers in the RTO's office. A length of approximately 75 feet situated between the booking hall and the footbridge was destroyed including the buffet, grill room and kiosk, dining car stores, hotels department central stores, RTO's office (formerly the ladies third class waiting room) and a number of the headquarters offices. In addition five bays of the station roof including three trusses were wrecked. The adjoining portion of the station buildings to the north for a length of about 60ft with the gentlemen's lavatories below the platform and a length of 190 ft to the south were seriously damaged. This latter portion included the enquiry office and the ladies first class waiting room and the headquarters offices situated above. The roof girders fell across the platforms blocking Nos 6, 7, 8 and 10 platforms. Measures were taken to strut the centre wall against any unbalanced steel ties across the undamaged span, to tie the centre wall to the main office block on the York Way side of the station.

The dread scene on 11th May 1940, after the night of bombing. The photographer is perched in the centre gutter of the roof, peering north westwards across the footbridge and Nos. 7, 8 and 10 platforms. The explosion took place only yards from the booking office and by a miracle two members of staff escaped serious injury ... but the office itself was wrecked, and millions of tickets, together with books, records, dating presses and all the paraphernalia of a large booking office were buried under debris. In pitch darkness, these two men made their escape from the wreckage, and then, badly shaken and with clothes torn, sat down for a while to consider how they should carry on the work which had been so suddenly interrupted. Apparently they decided that the passengers for the next train must be booked somehow, though even they could not shut their eyes to the fact that the virtual disappearance of their office and all that was in it presented some difficulty. However there was another office near by, very much smaller and not equipped with the requisite tickets, and with no staff on duty. They decided to install themselves there. They scoured surrounding offices for excess ticket books and blankcards, and, with the aid of the staff who came on duty later, the first morning train was successfully booked. **The locomotive, N2 No. 4761 (it was dragged out and subsequently repaired and was not finally withdrawn until 1960) was standing in No.10 platform. The Georgian Tea Room was chosen for the new booking office and passengers were being served within 36 hours. A report a fortnight or so later, on 27th May detailed progress ...** *Nos. 7 and 8 platforms are fully in use again but No. 6 is available only northwards from the footbridge as the strutting overlaps the platform track opposite the damaged area. No. 10 platform road is clear but is being utilised to accommodate the vehicles clearing the debris from No. 10 platform. In the destruction of the booking office the whole of the ticket stock was either lost or had to be scrapped and an entirely new stock of tickets is now in use. All the cash in the safe in the main line booking office, about £3-4,000, was recovered and there was very little loss of loose cash. The tea room on No. 10 platform is being used as a temporary booking office and is proving fairly satisfactory although there has been a certain amount of congestion. The enquiry work is at present being conducted in the seat reservation section of the enquiry office but it is hoped the remainder of the office will be available for use in a few days time. A buffet car has been placed at the south end of No. 10 platform for the sale of light refreshments to passengers and is being well patronised. Temporary arrangements have been made for the restaurant car stores and for the preparation of meals. Approximate estimate of the cost of restoration of the above work is £121,000; one locomotive, eleven coaches and four other vehicles were damaged − estimated cost of repairs is between £1,500 and £2,000.* **The sign, 'Hit back' could not be better sited.**

(Alec Swain Coll.)

The 'ole with preparatory work for renewal, on 17th November 1946. 'Temporary Arrangements' made for the comfort of passengers comprised these simple shelters, put up with old rail and spare girders. The roof was rebuilt more or less in the original style of the station the following year, though not before several alarming schemes for complete rebuilding had emerged from various dark corners ... it is an odd tale, buried in obscure minutes with an increasingly covert air. The tender for repair work, the culmination of extensive discussions stretching back over much of the previous year, had been accepted in May 1946 from Samuel Butler & Co. of the Albion Works, Stanningley, Leeds, at a cost of £11,738.1s.0d. The LNER was unable to enforce a penalty clause 'due to the uncertain position of steel supplies' ... Butler's appointment was odd, for on 4th July 1945 W.H.Johnson, 'Secretary, LNER', had accepted Messrs. Johnson Bros. tender, 'for sheeting glazing slating and boarding to the four bays of the western span of the Kings Cross Main Roof' at £4,762 – then on 26th October, with 'Sir Ronald W. Matthews in the chair' ... discussions took place regarding the 'Committee appointed in August to consider the question of the reconstruction of the roof at Kings Cross. The Board decided that the portion of the roof destroyed by enemy action should be replaced at an estimated cost of £21,000'. On 28th August 1945 consideration was deferred and by September no less than six schemes were submitted, mostly involving umbrella awnings and ranging from £180,000 to £235,000, 'to replace the portion destroyed by enemy action'. FitzHerbert Wright writes to Johnson the Secretary, from his Invicta Works at Grantham on 6th September 1945, recalling his comments at the meeting ... 'my view with regard to the station is that we should spend as little as possible now in view of the plans there are in the future such as electrification etc. This means in other words that I am in favour of repairing the hole in the station which I believe with the Government contribution will cost the company £10,000.' In August 1945 there was considerable discussion about 'removal of smoke' and 'the new station' (note the term), it was determined, 'should be like the LMS portion of Leeds City'. The committee argued over the precise meaning of 'clerestory' deciding that 'it is more applicable to ecclesiastical premises' – the talk further ranged on 'the concrete roof' proposed at Marylebone. All this is headed private and confidential... *On 22nd August 1945 it was decided that 'the present roof of the Kings Cross station ... be replaced by roof of more modern design, this includes umbrella roof in reinforced concrete'. Lord Balfour of Burleigh had written to Johnson on 31st July 1945; the good lord was interested to know 'the possibility that someday the roofs may have to accommodate overhead electrified stock.' This is underlined by Johnson .. 'I wonder whether all the possibilities of future air traffic have also been taken into account' – was he serious? – 'it may be that such has been ruled out ex-hypothesis and in such case will be considered at Lloyds Bank' (where he writes from – he was also a Director). Hopes are expressed in July 1945 about* doing away with the expensive arch span *upon which maintenance costs are so high; private rooms are booked in July 1945 for a meeting, unusually and pointedly declared private, confidential etc. and a lot of people suddenly can't make it, they're on holiday or doing something else. After this there is nothing, until the simple repair tender of the Albion Works, which started off this section above. Samuel Butler's sign announces the work and the local crane, presumably made available to the contractor, stands alongside.*

(Camden Libraries)

To all the great stations of Britain the War brought the tramp of service feet, unfamiliar uniforms and weapons and unheard-of accents. Yorkshire, Geordie and Scots were familiar enough at Kings Cross but with the enormous increase of service journeys in the Second World War, French, Poles, Norwegians, Canadians, Americans and many others (including German and Italian!) made Kings Cross amongst the most cosmopolitan in the country. Its awkward layout, the narrow inadequate concourse and the concentration of facilities on one side tested the place severely.

14 Ash Green,
Baldwin's Hill,
LOUGHTON, Essex.

EJH/CH.   5th January, 1943.

The Rt. Hon. Winston Churchill,
10, Downing Street,
LONDON. S.W.

Sir,

In 1941 a female relative of mine who, like many thousands of our young women, had the cause of Great Britain at heart, enlisted voluntarily in the W.R.N.S. and was sent to serve in Scotland.

She has been home to London on leave on various occasions, and upon each visit her experiences in travelling have been such that I feel it incumbent upon someone to place these disgusting experiences before you, although the appalling spectacles need to be seen to be believed, and as I only see the departure from London I will only deal with that.

On each occasion it is necessary to be at King's Cross for the 10.15 p.m. train two hours before it leaves; this is necessary if she is to get on the train at all, and then it is a case of fighting one's way in among drunken sailors, soldiers, etc., who frequently fight on the platform.

On the last occasion, December 29th, it was impossible to get on to the train at all; this meant remaining with many hundreds of people until 8.30 a.m. and although we managed to push her into the train it was only to stand, jammed in a corner, where she remained standing until 3.15 p.m. when she collapsed. On this occasion I saw a girl member of the A.T.S. knocked completely under the train, and I also heard a Canadian remark that in no country had he seen women treated in such a despicable manner.

I am wondering if there is any liaison between the number of people sent on leave and the number that the Railway Company can handle. I am also wondering why, if there can be so many compartments labelled "Officers only" there cannot be some compartments for women only. I wonder, too, how we can be expected to absorb all these splendid "knobs of sugar" concerning the postwar Europe if this is Britain's consideration for her grand fighting women, but above all I wonder if you can have the matter investigated, not by asking for the Railway Company's report, but actually investigated and, I hope, improved.

It is regretted that I have to burden you on this subject; you are obviously a busy man, but you are also Parliamentary representative for this constituency.

Yours faithfully,

(Sgd.) E.J. Hallett.

C. H. NEWTON
CHIEF GENERAL MANAGER

R. BELL
ASSISTANT GENERAL MANAGER

TELEPHONE WHITWELL 76

TELEGRAPHIC ADDRESS
"NEWTON, H.Q.1, L.N.E.R., HITCHIN"

REFERENCE

Letters to be addressed

THE CHIEF GENERAL MANAGER
LONDON & NORTH EASTERN RAILWAY
H Q 1 (VIA HITCHIN)

20th January, 1943.

W.

THE R.E.C.

604/215.   CONDITIONS AT KING'S CROSS.

In reply to your letter of the 19th January, there are few complaints about overcrowding on the Main Line trains from King's Cross and as a general rule passengers are carried in reasonable comfort except at holiday times.

The 10.15 pm. from King's Cross, which consists of 20 vehicles, usually has a load slightly in excess of the seating capacity. The Superintendent has gone personally into the working of this train and his report is quoted below :-

"This train offers an attractive service for points beyond Newcastle, and knowing the position passengers tend to arrive at King's Cross some time before the booked departure in order to obtain a seat, a practice which it would be very difficult and hardly reasonable to prevent. Loading figures and my enquiries, however, indicate that seats are usually available until shortly before departure time, after which passengers, if they wish to travel, must of necessity stand. The occasions on which standing room has been completely occupied are relatively few.

A number of incidents have arisen from time to time with passengers the worse for drink, but the position has not become serious nor beyond the capacity of the staff to control. Servicemen are largely concerned and the presence and prompt action of the Military Police has generally proved sufficient to avoid any serious difficulty."

The direction of M.W.T. about extra trains during the Christmas holidays covered 29th December. On that day three down relief trains only were allowed to the 10.5 am., 1 pm. and 3.30 pm. expresses for Edinburgh, Leeds and Newcastle respectively. From the early evening of the 29th large numbers of passengers for the North thronged King's Cross Station. A large proportion consisted of members of H.M. Forces. The 7 pm. to Aberdeen carried 1,900 passengers and the 10.15 pm. to Edinburgh 1,950. At mid-night about 700 passengers were still at the station and had to wait for the early morning trains. There was no train at 8.30 am. on December 30th, the nearest train to that hour being the 9.50 am. There is no record of a member of the A.T.S. being knocked under a train on either the 29th or 30th December and an accident of that nature would have been reported to the Company.

Our people have the closest possible liaison with the military authorities, but it is not our practice to label compartments "officers only". On the night expresses compartments are labelled "For women only", but are not fully used. On the 10.15 pm. train from King's Cross "Women Only" third class accommodation is provided for 28 passengers and only twice during December was this fully utilised, on December 29th and one other occasion. Rarely have the compartments been more than three-quarters full and frequently less than ten passengers have been seated therein, whilst the remainder of the train has been full.

Anyone like Mr. Hallett's relative, who is not prepared to "rough it" as the vast majority of people did at the end of the year, would be well advised not to travel during the holiday season.

p. C. H. NEWTON   R Bell

By the time of this view, 19th January 1945, the bombing was long over, though flying bombs and rockets were a terrible fear — a doodlebug had blocked the main line at Wood Green less than a week previously and in June 1944 one of these 'pilotless aircraft' had descended upon Tiber Street off York Way, shattering windows in Kings Cross and bringing down ceilings in No. 1 block of the general offices. Britain and the capital wore a battered look and St. Pancras, beyond, was only one amongst many stations (York was another notable victim) to lose its glazing. There was nevertheless hope in the air and a firmness in the step.

(Camden Libraries)

Wartime No. 10 platform, prior to the May 1942 bombing.

Greatcoated Britain, a chill January after a lean Yule, 1945.

(Copenhagen Coll.)

January 1945. This was the unprepossessing approach to one of the principal transport gateways of Britain, a muddle of huts and run-down buildings.

(Copenhagen Coll.)

South west corner of the station in January 1945. The squat cabin behind the policeman (the scene here, indeed in these few pages, is almost straight from The Ladykillers − *catch it on TV next time) is the season ticket office, no less.*

(Copenhagen Coll.)

Booking Hall and entranceway off 'Station Approach', alongside the west of the terminus. A Second World War view in the summer of 1942: note the uniforms, lady porters and wartime posters as well as the unfortunately Nationalsozialistische *visage of one of the porters.*

The Next Train .. it would have been easy to overlook the train *indicators at Kings Cross, such were the dense thickets of posters and signs, and the mild perversities of the platform arrangements. Once discovered they were straightforward but where this example stood is not quite clear. It is probably 1942, to judge from the LNER blackout curtain and the luggage and parcel racks possibly give a clue to the location.*

(National Railway Museum)

The traditional block characters of the station signwork had been turned over to the LNER favourite, the Gill Sans, in the early 1930s and these endured to fairly recent times. This is 'the Bravington Showcase', a wartime view of 15th July 1942. Set in the wall is the 1914-1918 Great Northern Railway War Memorial

(National Railway Museum)

The Great Northern Hotel, from the station roof. It is a fine building and a further (and now threatened) strange contrast between the two great terminus stations. Its interior, at least until the 1970s, was almost exotic, a warren of corridors, a soft deep piled womb of a place suffused with a peculiar *redness*. At least that is how it lingers in the mind years after, under admittedly peculiar circumstances. The Hotel had been built by Jay, the contractor, but the GN Board had examined at least one alternative, a proposal of Wednesday 27th March 1850 from a Mr.Vanlini 'of the London Hôtel, Albemarle Street, offering to take over the Refreshment Rooms at Peterborough and to build an Hôtel on the Company's ground at the London Terminus provided that he be allowed as the tenant on a lease of both'. Vanlini does not appear to have been successful in his endeavours for on Tuesday 4th May 1852 Jay enters again. He was 'prepared to build an Hôtel to cost £20,000 at the Kings Cross terminus'. The Board required that he confer with Mr. Lewis Cubitt and Jay later 'attended, with plans', on 18th May. The Hotel would 'be made fireproof, at an extra cost of about £1,000 … would let works without delay and would take measures …' On 17th August 1852 The Board heard from Lewis Cubitt that the work would cost £1,600 more, if 'Ancaster stone is used for the external Quoins, cornices and dressings instead of brick and cement'. Cubitt 'thought he ought not to recommend it.'

(Camden Libraries)

Inside the station. The west side remained wholly different in character from the east, bustling and cosmopolitan even, in comparison. The slight differences in the three girders beyond the bookstall betray the post-war replacements by Butler for the bombed 'ole; the period, to judge from the Type 2 diesel, is the early 1960s.

(National Railway Museum)

BR in lights — high hopes of 1949.

Classic Kings Cross departure, behind Quicksilver *on 21st August 1956. Despite all the fiddling about the terminus remained backward in terms of its signalling and track arrangements. The roller blind displaying '2' also bore a '3', on which it never stopped.*

(D.W.Hawkins)

The Cross on 2nd August 1955, with B1 4-6-0 No. 61093.

(B.K.B.Green)

Pacific backing down into platform 6, in a typical movement that punctuated the Kings Cross day. Beyond lies Goods Way and the goods depot and on the skyline the 'Ebonite' tower, actually a factory chimney.

(D.W.Hawkins)

Kings Cross on 11th August 1952. The quarters of the 'passenger loco' were luxurious (if noisy) in comparison with 'Top Shed' and well appointed. The B1 is in place as the main line pilot, ready as substitute; crewed by top link men on a rest week, it could stand there all day (this device spread the mileage bonuses).

(D.W.Hawkins)

Inviting interior. The famous clock came from the Great Exhibition, which figured so large in the earliest days of the terminus. Various stories have been woven about the clock and its bells; it had four faces (though the rear one was long ago neglected) and according to Johns was the only public striking clock installed at a railway terminus in Great Britain. It struck regularly for many years in a fashion described variously in the different accounts. A scribbled note on one of a bundle of Kings Cross papers and rebuilding plans at the Public Record Office reads: The station clock was removed from the Great Exhibition Building in Hyde Park 1851. The bells which sounded the hours and quarters were silenced in World War 1 and were taken down and melted in World War 2.

(Nocturne)

Platforms 7 and 8, originally built in 1926 as a narrow (12ft) concrete island. In 1938 its width had been increased to more sensible proportions. The LNER Magazine relates: 'A widening of the narrow island platform accommodating Nos. 7 and 8 platforms from 12½ to 24ft by absorbing No. 9 siding has relieved heavy congestion on these two platforms, where the intermixing of entraining and detraining passengers frequently led to restricted movement and confusion. A staircase is to be provided to the footbridge from the south side, and the widening of the platform will enable a lift connection to be made to the new subway for parcels and mails. Accommodation was found elsewhere for the rolling stock usually stabled temporarily in No.9 siding'. Most of the stock here is in maroon, rather than 'blood and custard' livery, suggesting the view is post-1956.

(Camden Libraries)

Platform 1 on 5th October 1938. The concentration of facilities along Platform 10 necessarily left this a neglected corner but the LNER was not unaware of the shortcomings of its Kings Cross terminus as a whole, comparing the place unfavourably to its other great London station, Liverpool Street. 'In comparison with Liverpool Street it is noticeable that at King's Cross there is very little circulating area and practically the whole of the public offices and rooms are concentrated along one platform (No. 10) which, by the way, is nearly 1,000 ft. long, whereas at Liverpool Street the area space is on a fairly generous scale and the various public services are spread over the entire head of the terminus'.

(National Railway Museum)

Along the east side ran what was originally (in part at least) the cab rank, latterly an access roadway for vehicles. It was not a salubrious place, by any means, the big surprise being that royalty used it regularly, coming in overnight from Balmoral.

(National Railway Museum)

Platform 1, in its more familiar role as parcels depot, 20th February 1963.

(National Railway Museum)

'Xmas Mail' on 1st December 1960.

(National Railway Museum)

Platform 10 and the Bravington's showcase. A fascinating illustration of parcels handling techniques at The Cross.

(National Railway Museum)

The main ticket office, decorated presumably for the Coronation of Elizabeth II.

(National Railway Museum)

Roof glazing at Kings Cross. Of the platform numbering the LNER Magazine *of 1938 would comment, a bit convolutedly: 'At King's Cross the sequence is broken between No. 1 and No. 10 because two of the reception lines which were so numbered have disappeared under schemes of improvement. Larger schemes of alterations at King's Cross concern the erection of a new building and a subway to certain platforms for facilitating the business of mails and parcels, and the important underground works at present being carried out by the Passenger Transport Board for facilitating passenger connections.' Grander developments even than this were in hand in 1938; parts of the place had been comprehensively dolled up but by the late 'fifties were showing signs of weariness. In 1938 an almost unrecognisable description of the place had been possible: 'Turning to the redecoration of the public rooms, much forethought was directed to schemes giving the maximum of cheerfulness and comfort. An entirely new first class ladies' waiting room bears the hall mark of an extremely comfortable lounge, having been decorated with the latest mural rexine, well carpeted and furnished with Lloyd Loom armchairs. Special toilet facilities adjoin. The third class ladies' room offers much the same degree of comfort, whilst the general room has been given a warmer and more inviting appearance. The mainline booking office and hall, in their turn, kept the decorators busy for some time, a new system of powerful lighting and indicator signs adding to a far more general atmosphere of brightness.'*

(National Railway Museum)

Roof gazing at Kings Cross. At none of the London terminus stations, it seemed (though this is a personal view) did the roof stretch up to such immeasurable heights, vaulting above the rather drab platforms and bridge below.

(National Railway Museum)

Entrance to 14 and 15 on 24th September 1956. The bulk and blankness of the western wall of the 'Local Station' only emphasised further the curious isolation of the 'far' suburban side. The photographs on this page and opposite chart more or less the spreading suburban platforms, from 11 to 17, demonstrating and confirming Jackson's apt description, Suburban Accretions

(L. Tibble–Hewitson Coll.)

It is unfortunately often a bit difficult to depict Kings Cross as other than a confused clutter inside or out. Odd parts like the east wall or platform 11 seen here, or even more markedly the so-called 17 on the western extremity of the station, seemed to the average observer more like workshops or stores. This is 5th October 1938, with some sort of work going on, probably new venting in connection with the improved Platform 10 rooms and offices (for this is the rear wall of the original west side of the terminus). The ubiquitous Kings Cross carts and trollies are present in their usual numbers and the Virol (it was a vitamin enriched food with a consistency rather like Marmite, especially popular for kids) kiosk is presumably one of the redundant pair destined as the LNER Magazine noted, for Liverpool Street ... 'Side issues connected with some of the improvements include the closing of the hotel long bar on No.10 platform at the end of February 1937, and the transfer of two displaced kiosks to Liverpool Street for services at that station. In addition to the various improvements, the lighting and indicator arrangements have been completely modernised, automatic machines grouped together, and advertisement panels re-arranged along more uniform and harmonious lines, the whole producing a much more orderly, brighter and pleasing terminus wherein assemble our world–famous trains ever ready to maintain the traditional slogan King's Cross for Scotland'. Our scene here hardly matches this latter slogan but this was in the nature of Kings Cross. It was a continuing theme and much of the improvement work of 1937-1938 was necessarily concerned with the station's shortcomings: 'Earlier stages of modernization of the various amenities and facilities along No. 10 platform were the provision of up to date inquiry and telegraph offices; a Georgian tea room to which an illuminated canopy has been added: the remodelling and enlargement of the buffet and restaurant, which also has been given an illuminated awning; the setting back of Messrs W.H. Smith & Son's bookstall and its reconstruction incorporating the latest ideas for service and display inside as well as out; the resiting and erection of a new tobacco and confectionery kiosk between the buffet and restaurant, which left a clearer entrance to the latter and, incidentally, concealed an unsightly goods lift entrance; the installation of the latest toilet conveniences; and the standardisation of the lower range of windows along the platform, combining a more pleasing design of framing ... further and subsequent alterations within the interior of the main building include the erection of new uniform platform barriers with illuminated numbers and showing train-departure timings, the withdrawal of an out of date train indicator on the footbridge, the re-siting and erection of a new sub-bookstall side by side and in tone with a new attractive fruit shop facing Nos 5 and 6 platforms, new ranges of telephone cabinets centralised inside the booking hall, a new letter-box with oak surround to harmonise with the improved surroundings (provided by the Post Office and re-sited to a position in front of the telegraph office) and the erection of two new attractive show-cases.'

Given all this it is something of a mystery that Kings Cross remained doggedly fixed in time, and a bit of a mess.

(L. Tibble–Hewitson Coll.)

The site of the old 'loco', long since transmuted into platforms and 'umbrella roof', and the Hotel Curve. Like the York Way platform here was a sort of twilight existence, the place only really coming to life in the evening rush. It never seemed to shake off the steam era and was very atmospheric even into the 1970s, Brush Type 2s powering their way out, wreathed in fume, complete with compartment, non-corridor stock. The waiting crowd eddied and surged with the often unpredictable disposition of compartments; those not already crowded usually, upon closer examination, turned out to be 'Ladies Only.'

(L. Tibble–Hewitson Coll.)

Wild Swan with the 'The Master Cutlers Special.' The vagaries of light and the brooding backdrop of the great train shed combine to highlight the mystical A4 curves.

(National Railway Museum)

42

Dominion of New Zealand bursts forth from Kings Cross. Pacifics, and especially the streamlined engines, came to personify The Cross in a way that the LMS Coronations, probably more impressive in power and bulk, could not do up the road at Euston. 'The Talisman' began on 17th September 1956, giving a 4pm departure from Kings Cross and from Edinburgh, on a 6hrs 40mins schedule with just one stop of six minutes at Newcastle. This was useful for passengers and change of crew, and a corridor tender was not necessary. The trains ran Mondays to Fridays and each included twin first class coaches from the pre-war Coronation trains, which also left at 4pm. From 17th June 1957 another pair of trains, also named 'The Talisman' began to run, at 7.45am from Kings Cross, and at 7.30 am from Edinburgh, with arrivals that enabled the coaches to return on the 4pm departures.

(National Railway Museum)

Leaving The Cross on 29th April 1952. For many years late departures plagued the working of the station, before new lines and tunnels alleviated matters. The cramped nature of the place left things ever tight however but as W. Rayner Thrower writes (Kings Cross in the Twenties), priority was always accorded the main expresses ... 'Nothing should interfere with the running of the profitable long distance trains, a concept remaining from the earliest days'.

(D.W.Hawkins)

Until the new 'passenger loco' was built the Kings Cross approaches were even more constrained and claustrophobic, an impression heightened after one's long descent through the many arches and bewildering galleries of Copenhagen and Belle Isle. Moves to purchase the site, a 'largely defunct gas works' (Great Northern Engine Sheds, Hooper and Griffiths, Irwell Press 1989) had begun before the First World War but it descended into something of a legal mire (see the above book for much greater detail regarding the various Kings Cross sheds) and a tender was not approved until the late part of 1922. There was a hiccup in the opening due principally to a wildly optimistic completion date and the new yard, known as 'bottom shed' or more commonly 'the passenger loco' came into use early in 1924. The offending wall incidentally, 'of the recessed type' had appeared in 1892 when the third Gas Works Tunnel was bored. It consisted of brick and concrete and its demolition was estimated to involve the removal of '2500 cubic yards of material from the site'.

(Railway Magazine)

Cock o' the North reverses past the new yard. This is the pioneer 2-8-2 and the occasion one of its numerous trials. The year is 1934. 2001 operated out of Doncaster from new in May, frequently visiting London until the end of July, when it moved to Scotland for the work intended for it.

(A.B.Collins Coll.)

A remarkable view of 'The Royal Twins', both the Cambridge 'Royal Clauds', at Kings Cross in the mid–1930s. 8783 on the left, by the office, is either coming off or going to a royal working (hence the four discs) and 8787 is standby. The royal family, like anybody else, could tire sometimes of formality, and apparently preferred The Cross to Liverpool Street for Sandringham visits. This avoided the ceremonials necessary upon entering the City of London, and the procession to Liverpool Street.

(A.B.Collins Coll.)

The passenger loco could be a hectic place, busier than many small depots about the system, though it was never classified so. The lightweight mechanical plant, subsequently familiar across the country, was a feature for which the LNER was largely responsible, being an innovator of such ideas in the 1920s. From Hooper & Griffiths … 'Improvements were not long in coming. In about 1928 a half-ton skip hoist coaling plant was installed at the southern end of the site and the original coaling platform removed.' This view is post-1934.

(A.B. Collins Coll.)

Flying Scotsman **on the Kings Cross 'table. Its corridor tender was removed from 1936.**

(Nocturne)

Kings Cross in one of its periodic volcanic moods.

(B.K.B.Green)

*The **RCTS** History describes the 'bold experiment' of May 1932 – five buffet expresses each weekday between Cambridge and Kings Cross and Clauds were frequently used, 'notably on 25th July 1932' when no less than three of the 4-4-0s were at the terminus.*
(Alec Swain Coll.)

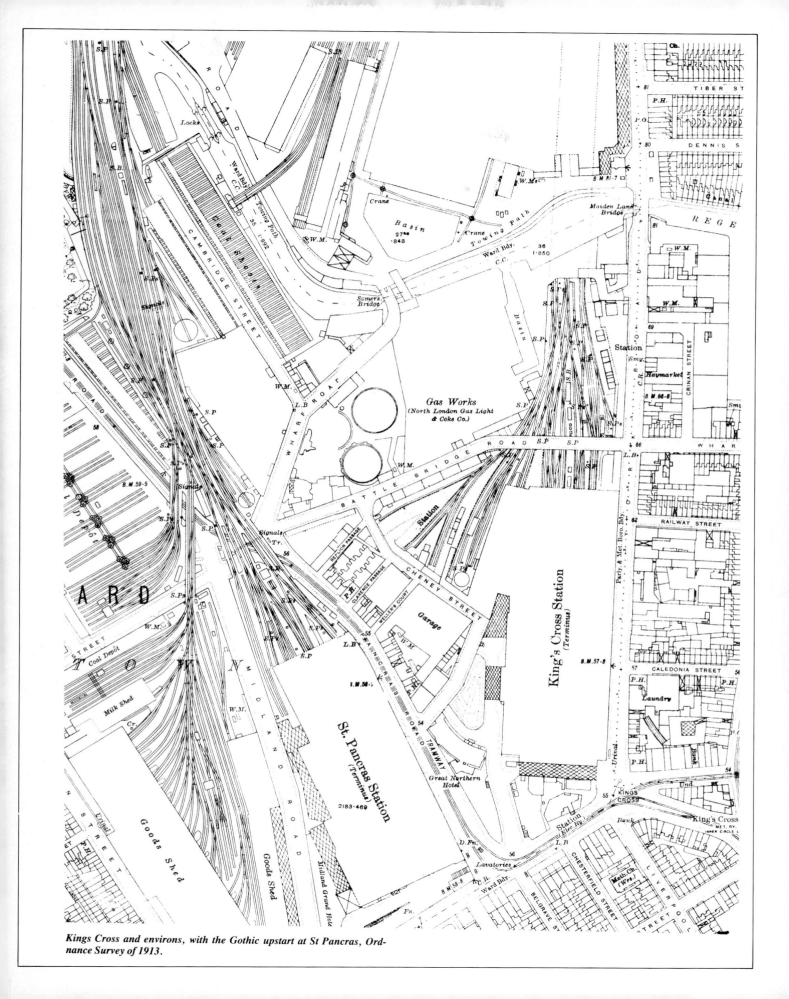

Kings Cross and environs, with the Gothic upstart at St Pancras, Ordnance Survey of 1913.

The hot seat at Kings Cross was, in proper ramshackle railway tradition, a crude and lonely hut, though the casually laid aside plate will probably prompt a sigh of regret from most of us. The passenger loco had a foreman throughout the 24 hours and a variety of other staff depending on the hour, day and season. A coalman was needed most of the time and a labourer for general work (he could fill a wagon of ash in little more than a day) whilst a procession of footplate staff signing on at 'Top Shed' made their way down as required, on an unofficial 'walk route' — a ladder down the Camley Street coal drops.

(The Thompson Society)

Activity at The Cross.

(J. Merry)

Sun Castle, one of the few engines habitually referred to by name amongst enginemen – in this case a vaguely obscene rendering chiefly concerned with a piece of anatomy crucial to much of traditional British humour. On the Kings Cross 'table, precisely the site of the 'recessed' retaining wall shown earlier. The turntable was a good 'un, in contrast to the Top Shed example.

(National Railway Museum)

The 'table and loco yard, together with the station, reduced to its simplest elements in the signalbox.

(National Railway Museum)

Bois Roussel off 'The Yorkshire Pullman'. The turntable is amongst the most familiar in British railway literature, easily recognisable through the (possibly unique) well wall, in steel rather than the usual brick. It figured prominently (with Sun Castle) in a publication of quite astonishing, and chastening, hope and optimism in 1951 – Your British Railways. Of the vacuum turntable it could declare: 'Oh! So easy. Modern turntables are worked from the locomotive's own brake pump. A simple connection and the driver and fireman had themselves to push the whole turntable and its hundred-ton load round.'

(National Railway Museum)

Seagull **in fiery mood.**

(National Railway Museum)

Sun Castle **again. Not by any means did all visiting engines call here, those from far afield ran out light to Top Shed whilst those using 'the passenger' generally hailed from sheds south of Doncaster.**

(National Railway Museum)

J50 on empty stock work in 1950. Kings Cross did not have pilots as such but 'shunt duties', often three of them. There were quiet periods of course enabling 'a kip up the spur' at night, mid-morning, or afternoon but this type of shunt duty was unusual on the LNER. It derived from the peculiarity of the job – it could be the best part of half a day's work for instance to take empty stock to Holloway sidings and get back.

(D.C.Conners)

June 1959, with Pacifics hurrying off; for shunting in out and around the terminus and yard engines were frequently coupled together.

(Derek Clayton)

Walter K. Whigham on 'The Talisman.' The 'blue 'uns' in especial (all A4s were so named whatever the colour) received personal attention and no effort was spared in time and money, particularly for the non–stop. The Talisman, London – Edinburgh and introduced in 1956, changed crews at Newcastle; it was still specially prepared but not to the extent of the non–stop. Coaling the latter could take some four hours, for wagons of special coal broken down by hand to brick size lumps to fill the voids could ease another three quarters of a ton into the tender. The Kings Cross–based A4s were renowned during these years for their fine condition, principally through the arrangement of The Top Shed shedmaster, P.N.Townend. They were certainly exceptional and a contrast for instance to the Gateshead examples, which were turned out in relatively shabby condition.

(Railway Covers)

*Flying Scotsman **in want of a lamp, in the early summer of 1959.***

(Derek Clayton)

*Deltic **on 7th July 1959. It had arrived early in the year to some success, despite periods out of use with radiator trouble, though being a single example, spares for minor problems would always have a disproportionate effect. It had returned to 'its usual Kings Cross–Doncaster diagram' on May 28th and in the first weekend of June it had gone to Scotland via the LMR for a weeks trial. Trains Illustrated **at the time lauded its feats, including 'the working of a 550–ton train over the 29·1 miles from Peterborough to Grantham in 25 minutes'. Deltic's stay at Hornsey 'had not been the most fruitful of its career so far'; tight clearances apparently had restricted it to a daily mileage well below potential, for it could not 'freely work beyond Doncaster'.***

(Diesel Days)

Bongrace **on 'The Flying Scotsman' – the Peppercorn A1s were worthy successors to the Gresley engines, though they were relatively unsung. The RCTS** History **recalls them as 'the least troublesome of any of the Doncaster designed Pacifics, running the greatest annual mileages and performing consistently well'.**

(Railway Covers)

67768 in August 1958. The shunt signal below the colour light was used when a simple local movement around the station yard was required.

(Derek Clayton)

Walter **again, on the 'non stop'.** *(Derek Clayton)*

Sir Ralph Wedgwood **and 67793 in June 1959.** *(Derek Clayton)*

Tanks at the local side on 7th March 1958.

The passenger loco and the Kings Cross approach, 10th January 1957. The engine yard was always in close touch with the home shed only a short walk away and a small delivery van (in LNER blue) could be dispatched with a variety of spare bits and pieces.

Above all the cavernous noise and turmoil of the Gas Works Tunnels the whole character of Kings Cross changed, to an older, more private, commercial world, much of it of ancient aspect. This is Goods Way, which fronted most of the goods depot and provided access to the entire site. Goods Way as we have seen was driven across the roof of the tunnels at right angles to the station. The various buildings fronted onto this oddly named thoroughfare and most can be picked out in the skyline in earlier views north from the terminus. The traffic remained persistently agricultural in nature; truly 'the lowly tuber' and its fellows made for the unique character of 'the goods' and a greater contrast to the station, with its principal trains of the Empire, can hardly be imagined. Not least among the traffic was an enormous volume of fodder for the Great Northern's horses; and those of the LNER, though from the 1930s this waned considerably. In a resolutely poor district security at 'the goods' was important, it employed hundreds of men and the canal, always known as 'the Cut' (it lies hidden beyond between 'the goods' and the gas holders) and the alleyways about made it difficult to police. Kids in the 1930s were drawn to its mysteries but were easily spotted and ejected. It was a place ineluctably of smells — smoke drifted in from the railway close by but it is remembered as a vast walled–in foodstore, a concentration and distillation of farmyard Lincolnshire, veg and horse manure. Horse carts of course were everywhere, replaced in the first instance by steam lorries, which could set light to the street cobbles round about (they were often tarred wooden blocks) when the fires were livened up; post-war any number of ex–service lorries flooded in to take over, together with British Railways' own vehicles. The large main goods shed for general traffic put up in the depot's very beginnings, close by the potato market, boasted a variety of rail approaches, inside, either side and across, linked by a series of cranes and turntables. In the late 1890s, the place greatly overtaxed, a new but rather smaller shed for down traffic 'the outward shed' was put up to the west, across the other side of the early coal yard. Tenders for 'The New Coal Yard and Goods Depot, London Goods Yard Kings Cross' were signed with the aptly named Charles Wall on 9th December 1897; at a cost of £56,503 it included an incline approach, retaining walls and coal drops/buildings on the site of the old coal yard between the old and new goods shed. The new 'outward shed' was to stand on the ancient 'coal and stone dock' and the whole of this, termed a 'barge basin' was to be pumped dry and 'efficent Temporary dams' erected across its opening to the Regents Canal. Before the new outward shed was put up (presumably in 1898) the old shed dealt with both inward and outward goods — complete trains of up to 30 wagons. The practice for years was simply to draw out a down train ready for its journey but 'growing complexity of traffic and the pressure with regard to competitive towns' saw an alteration to the work, with individual trucks turned out over 'tables from each platform to waiting trains in the parallel sidings. They were then dispatched 'within short intervals of each other instead of the former lengthened waits between.' The new down goods shed eased much of the difficulty 'and trucks for all parts of the Great Northern system are now loaded up simultaneously and dispatched in rapid relays to Clarence Yard, Holloway, for marshalling into the through trains for the West Riding, Manchester, Liverpool, Ireland, and the Lancashire district, Scotland and the North Eastern line, Nottingham and Derbyshire, Staffordshire and the potteries, Norwich, Yarmouth, and the north Norfolk district, with of course Lincolnshire and the home counties, including such desirable nursery grounds for business as Cambridge, Luton, etc.'

(National Railway Museum)

Hogarthesque picture of the potato market, from The Illustrated Times, said to be 1864.

The Tuber's Tale

The Kings Cross goods station and yard is older than the present station. For farm produce, coal and livestock, it was probably unrivalled in the capital. The humble potato lay at the heart of its greatness; it was an ancient trade which had nurtured the urban poor of England as much as any number of Irish peasants. Contemporary developments were noted in the *Illustrated Times;* the big London potato market had been at Tooley Street, Borough, and vessels laden with vegetables came to Thames wharves from all over the eastern coast. This coasting trade was soon directed almost entirely to the Great Northern. From *The Leisure Hour: If we go up Maiden-lane to what was formerly the passenger station of the Great Northern Railway, we shall come upon it, and witness a spectacle calculated to excite ideas on the subject of potatoes such as few people are accustomed to entertain. The old station itself constitutes the market into which numerous lines of rails converge each and all of them loaded with huge trams or potato vans of a peculiar construction, and built for this especial traffic. They have wide trap doors and wide folding doors at the side, for the convenience of unloading. Each one will contain some six or eight tons of tubers which are shot in in bulk, without sacks and their unloading and sacking employs a considerable staff of men, who work continuously from one week's end to another. The number of vans must amount to several hundreds; they cover several acres of ground, and as they stand in all directions, on the main-ways, sidings, and turntables, they show like an irregular town of small houses in the labyrinths of which one might easily become bewildered and lost. The surrounding buildings, once the offices and waiting rooms for tickets and passengers have been changed into depots and market houses crammed with plethoric sacks and the platform itself is heaped up with them, almost to the obstruction of the gangway. In addition to this, lofty brick edifices have arisen on the surrounding land to serve as warehouses for the salesman and potato-factors to whom the several cargoes are consigned by the growers. The quantity of potatoes sold in this market varies from 700 or 800 to as much as 1,000 tons per week and occasionally we are informed, in times of crises or anticipated dearth, almost doubles that amount.*

Almost any of the 'dull roots' which could be produced in eastern England came to Kings Cross and the Great Northern traffic grew on the essential requirements of the city — coal for heat, vegetables and meat. This had all been foreseen though its rapid growth took the company by surprise. The Islington Cattle Market Co. had been in touch as early as the summer of 1849 with a prospectus and a request 'for the Board towards promoting this undertaking'. 'Consideration was deferred' but by June 1850 Cubitt was instructed 'to report without delay on land for the cattle station at the Caledonian Road'. The London cattle traffic whilst 'cognate to the subject of Kings Cross' (was not) 'in exact relation to it'. J. Medcalf, retired Out Door Goods Manager, (he began his career at the temporary passenger station) rightly however points out the pioneering qualitites of the Great Northern with respect to it .. 'in the lasting interests we may hope, of the people of London'.

The hopes and plans of the 'Islington Cattle Co.' were eventually made real through the agency of the Corporation and when the great cattle market was erected on Copenhagen Fields the GN was ideally placed for the business. Three of its four gin palaces (there was a pub at each corner) and its central clock tower stand there still.

Medcalf had a keen sense of the ridiculous (probably the prime essential for the management of a place like Kings Cross Goods) and in his retirement he followed his first *Railway Magazine* writings by an unusual account, 'Kings Cross Goods Station'; of the cattle traffic he recalls: *direct connection was quickly made by means of the Holloway unloading pens and a private road leading straight to the market. In this way, no other railway company having similar access, we may fairly say countless droves of 'Durhams' 'Shorthorns', 'Teviots', and the rest have found their way to the stomachs of 'Her Majesty's faithful beefeaters' (meaning the entire population, barring vegetarians) to say nothing of untold myriads of sheep, pigs and such like ' small deer'. 'Improvements' have eaten up the old private way, but the stock still have the nearest access to the great market by crossing the Caledonian Road.'*

Black Jem's **successors.** *(see page 67)*

The Kings Cross traffic was enormously valuable as well as of prodigious quantity. Medcalf talks of the bewildering variety of size, shape and handling requirements — from a container of theatrical props 40ft long 'to a tiny box of spring flowers.' Bales, trusses, packs, 'a hogshead of tobacco there, a small tin of oil here, washing and wringing machines, light castings, bags of nails, pumps, marble mantels, iron bedsteads, huge bales of paper, and a mountainous heap of wicker-work chairs'.

The potato market, remarkable not the least for its exotic arrangement of wagon tables. The humble nature of the principal produce is seen to be matched by the wholly prosaic quality of the market itself. Goods depots have always been severely neglected places from the standpoint of railway study, through the closed off and shut away nature of the operations involved; they were always difficult of access and lacked the obvious attraction of locomotives ... The Great Northern Railway has conferred a benefit upon the middle and lower classes of London, of which most of them are not fully aware. The railway brings to them a constant and invariable supply of a species of food indispensable to them all, and by so doing has for some time kept the price from undergoing those fluctuations, which at various periods in former years have brought the very poor to the threshold of famine.

(Camden Libraries)

Enormous quantities of potatoes travel the whole distance from Scotland and the mass is made up by contributions from the various stations and depots between Middlesex and the north of the island. Looking at the place, its odd curves and openings, eccentric trackwork and potato sacks hanging up to dry like Monday's washing, it is easy to nod agreement at Medcalf's description, 'something of a mosaic, additions and alterations having been made from time to time'. The potato market fronted York Road 'while to the eastward there is the ... Caledonian Road, with its mud, its shabby frontages and its fish and vegetable stalls, with their naphtha flare lamps at night,'

(National Railway Museum)

Mr. Plimsoll's coal shoots. Camley Street lies in a deep trough, out of sight to the right. At Kings Cross there was indeed a vast bulk of potatoes, grain, stone and bricks, timber and deals, hay and straw, as we have seen, and above all, coals. Above all coals, certainly, and with an industrial commercial and domestic market as vast as London, the yards were extensive from the first. By the early 1860s there was already at Kings Cross an enormous spread of coal stacking ground, yards and staithes and 'drops', or 'shoots'. Kings Cross by the 1890s was working a gross annual tonnage of over one million, exclusive of coal worked through subsidiary depots at Finsbury Park, Poplar, Hackney Wick and south London. The whole lot, bricks to broccoli, was a daunting business of 'picking out'. All the various commodities, potatoes, coal or whatever, all had their separate dealers, all screaming for attention. The handling of coal in particular was rendered easier by the shoots shown here, reached by a bridge over the Canal to Cambridge (later Camley) Street 'put up by Mr. Plimsoll, the former M.P for Derby, and worked by horse-power and traversers, has furnished the trade with a quick and easy means of supplying their wants, and these drops have recently come into the direct possession of the Company by the expiring of a lease'.

(Camden Libraries)

Looking west into the shoots, from the access bridge over 'the cut'; Camley Street lies in a deep trough out of sight beyond. The carriages are passing on the Midland main line into St. Pancras.

(Camden Libraries)

The shoots, or drops as they were known in later years, were built up in brick — wagons were emptied into it and traders took delivery on road vehicles from this malodorous accessway between the drops and the canal or directly from the other, Camley Street side. The coalman placed a sack at the end of the drop, shutting off the supply when it was filled.

(Camden Libraries)

Top of the shoots. Wagons appear to have moved on the 'traverser way' by a bizarre system of trollies, an exraordinary device powered, it would seem, by overhead cables. From the plans it will be clear that Mr. Plimsoll's depot grew in size and complexity and certainly the positioning (and possibly the number) of the traversers altered accordingly. Beyond, the outline of a further trolley, on a central traverser, can just be determined.

(Camden Libraries)

Trolley and burden in position — a standard steel open wagon, safe on the cradle-like device, in a remarkable manoeuvre high above the yards, canals, chimneys and roofs of Kings Cross. Its operation would seem to have been something of a wobbly one and its slow procession across the Kings Cross skyline must have been a wondrous sight.

(Camden Libraries)

Kings Cross on 2nd December 1947, the motive power depot water softener looming beyond.
(Camden Libraries)

The goods yard on 19th December 1947, apparently from a position perched atop the water softener. Most striking is the sheer variety of traffic even some 50 years after Medcalf's first description. Hordes of men worked here, unsurprisingly given the labour intensive nature of the task, the incessant changeover of goods from wagon to cart and lorry, lifting, hauling and carrying off. So it was that Kings Cross goods played a great part in the economy of the grim streets round about. It had been bad in the 1930s and life was still very hard in this part of London (and across much of Britain in what we now term the inner city) at the end of the 1940s. Incendaries, HE flying bombs and rockets had littered the area in the Second World War and by December 1947 (a particularly severe winter), austerity and shortages were taking a toll. In the Kings Cross district of the 1940s child prostitution already enjoyed a long pedigree though the worst effects of poor nutrition had paradoxically been largely assuaged by the war – those who remained got a better balanced diet and those who went to war, apart from the obvious dangers, enjoyed light, air, decent food and a vermin-free bed for the first time in their lives. Copenhagen Street was typical; a local cobbled way leading off York Road opposite the potato market, there was a noisome underground wrought iron public toilet, a puzzle to many residents – who in their right mind would think to use it? and uncomfortably obvious in hot summers. Bed bugs made summer nights in Copenhagen Street additionally unpleasant, small boys swam 'the cut' (useful also for drowning cats) to steal and eat locust beans (intended for cattle feed) from barges, and adults, particularly old ladies, habitually urinated in the gutter. Families lived more or less communally in the tenements, the bed legs standing in paraffin pots to foil the vermin. In time the bugs learned to drop off the ceilings. The landlords, to pack more tenants in, had extended many of the homes forward to take up the tiny gardens. Done on the cheap, the original front steps were simply left in position in the new 'hallways' so that they ran on two levels under the rebuilt houses. Boadicea was long believed (probably erroneously) to have fought a battle on this site and Wat Tyler's gathering is recorded on a plaque.

(Camden Libraries)

Ever after traffic on the 'Caley' at this point was punctuated by the nervous herds, hoofs clattering and sliding on the mean cobbles. Ever and anon one bold animal would burst free to ensuing chaos, only to be run to earth in one of the numerous alley workshops roundabout, to the great consternation of all. Like all the Kings Cross work, it was subject to great fluctuation: *when the company in turn with its competitors gets the whole of certain Scotch traffic, the work goes on, through the pens and up the lane, 'from morn till noon, and noon to dewy eve', as though the universe were resolving itself into a chaos of mutton and pork, horns and hoofs, and ribs and sirloins.*

The 'chaos of mutton and pork' brought an unmistakable agricultural air to this part of London. Horses and the by-products thereof were everywhere, heaps of vegetables trundled by in carts, straw flew in the breeze, the sharp sweetness of manure hung in the air and foreign brown clay washed from the potatoes to lodge in every crevice.

Coal seems to have pre-dated the vegetable trade into Kings Cross; doubtless the two traffics waxed alongside each other but they did not simply fall into the waiting lap of the Great Northern. Medcalf again:

Very naturally the most ample provision has always been made and now exists at King's Cross for dealing with coal traffic. 'Coal' has been a sort of watchword of the Great Northern ever since their great fighting chairman, Mr. Beckett Denison, put his back to the wall, and kept it there, session after session, with the determination to show that his railway was, amongst other things, a great coal carrying line, and that neither colliery combinations nor the schemes of rival managers, James Allport, Edward Watkin, Captain Huish, and the rest, should prevent the Company realising its destiny. King's Cross was the first great coal depot set up by a Railway Company for the supply of this now indispensable mineral to the inhabitants of London, 'vice' the sea route in great measure 'displaced'. It may be remembered that when merchants showed backwardness in coming forward to support the Great Northern, the latter grasped it's nettle by buying coal and arranging for its disposal in the metropolis through the agency of Mr. Herbert Clarke, a brother of the then General Manager, who for years was about the largest coal merchant in the world. The arrangement had to be superseded eventually, but its object was fully attained. Barriers were broken down in all directions, monopolies and privileges were broken up and a free flow of the coal traffic secured for London and its immediate neighbourhood. The name of 'Herbert Clarke, Limited' still shows up amongst the coal sidings and offices at King's Cross like a battle-stained banner, the relic from some half forgotten war. When the first few trucks of coal began to trickle into King's Cross, just about 50 years ago, few could have thought the trade would ever reach the dimensions of the present day. The Midland Railway did not exist in London, the London and North Western were then too 'orty' to bother about 'coals' and the then Eastern Counties were very much of a 'negligible quantity'.*

Coal drops were in operation more or less from the first and on 4th January 1852 Mr. Child the 'Manager of the Coal Traffic, London District' reported to the Board upon the case of a coal labourer 'injured at the Coal Drops on 6th December 1852 when a coal waggon fell through the roof into the mess room while the men were at dinner, and who subsequently died of measles. [?!] The parents are now in great distress.' They were given £5 but Kings Cross was already a workplace of hazards; at the same meeting £10 was awarded to the widow of labourer John Keating, killed in the station on 14th December 1852.

The potato market grew up alongside York Way above the main line tunnel, on the eastern margin of the goods station.

Earliest mention seems to have been in April 1853 in a Report from the General Manager, recommending a 'line of potato warehouses with two floors, estimated cost £2,000 to be erected in time for the next season in the Goods Station at Kings Cross.' This was duly sanctioned by the Board which approved a further £820 a few days later for 'a third floor'. By the end of the century the gross total of goods of all kinds was already close to a million tons a year *exclusive* of coal and of course livestock — dealt with up the road. A contract was let on 18th September 1896 for the re-roofing of the potato market, costed at £8,778; 'the extension of the roof covering the present potato sidings at the back of the warehouses, the covering of the roadway between the front of the warehouses and the York Road and other works'. Andrew Handyside of Derby was the successful contractor. There were '35 to 40' potato traders in late GN days and 28 by about 1930. By that time according to Christopher Maughan (*The Markets of London, Pitman 1931*) there were 39 warehouses, the tenants all well known as vegetable growers or merchants 'or in both capacities, and there is a long waiting list of applicants. Only lack of space prevents the construction of further warehouses for the trade at this particular centre'. A line of track extended the whole length of the potato market termed, Maughan relates, 'the 10 o'clock Road', from its long association with a night goods. Wagons, up to 130 of them, were transferred off turntables into the warehouses, each accommodating two, three or four. The warehouses were 'the finest now extant' though Medcalf was well aware that the place lacked beauty and classic lines. Comparison with the Regents Canal ('with its top dressing of London slime') to Venice was, he rightly felt .. 'too poetic' a bias. The potato wagons, the roots packed in 1 cwt bags, were turned daily into each merchant's wagon to disappear in greengrocer's vans, coster's carts and the like 'into the capacious stomach of London.'

Even the great goods shed proved inadequate to its task and in the early years of the new century was turned over to 'inwards' goods only, with 'outwards' dealt with at new premises on the site of the coal basin.

The level of traffic could be quite astounding, the various peaks and fluctuations due to weather and crop failure being reckoned in 'scores of thousands of tons'. On occasion there might be a thousand wagons of potatoes (Medcalf calls it 'this homely root') standing in and about Kings Cross. It was an incessant task to sort this lot and moving the wagons desired by each trader involved an astonishing endless round of capstan and engine shunting work. Medcalf dryly paid tribute to the energy of the GN staff which enabled this work to be conquered season by season, 'with a moderate amount of patience and courtesy on the part of the merchants'. One of the best capstanmen in the country was to be found at Kings Cross 'a mulatto nearly as black as a negro' and ex-sailor held in great regard, 'Black Jem'.

The potato market remained open 'the whole day' in earlier years and from about 5 am to about 4 pm by the 1930s. *The Leisure Hour* described our root with some exactness as 'not very ornamental'. The buyers attended, it was pointed out, really according to conditions elsewhere and when foreign potatoes arrived on the River the GN warehouses would be 'relatively deserted.' It was a state of affairs however 'which never lasts long, the reaction comes with the exhaustion of the sea borne cargoes and then the tide of potato dealers sets in again for the new market. The market opens at an early hour but it is not unusual to see the approaches swarming with vehicles of every kind before the gates are thrown open.'

haughty?

67

Brighter days – 1st July 1960 and York shed's Balmoral prepares for its journey north with the 'Tees Tyne Freighter', the collapse of railway goods levels as yet unguessed at.

(National Railway Museum)

Likely enough a denizen of Copenhagen Street or some equivalent, demonstrating use of a pinch bar in the engine shed yard, on 26th January 1953.

(National Railway Museum)

Cleaning gang at Kings Cross, the bowler hat presumably marking out its chief.

(Alec Swain Coll.)

Night work on the 4-6-4, No. 10000.

(Alec Swain Coll.)

Engines inside the repair shop, the central part of the old 'Crescent' engine shed.

(National Railway Museum)

A stroll from York Way round the perimeter of the yard brought one to the motive power depot offices. The vast structure alongside is the water softener on its base; passing to the right took you to the first sidings and the growing sound of engines, then to the obscurely named area of the depot, 'The Continent'.

(National Railway Museum)

This eight road conventional engine shed was up in front of the Crescent in 1862: it was originally possessed of a roof with transverse pitches but was rebuilt by British Railways in 1949. The place was always chronically overcrowded and preparation pits were provided on the north side, served by a water gantry visible beyond. 'Top Shed' has exercised a fascination over the years out of all proportion to its size, a fame rooted in some judicious 1930s and 1950s publicity, some finely written accounts of the place and of course the majestic quality of its locomotives; amongst the most renowned in the country, they powered some of Britain's best trains through the prestige years of the LNER and British Railways in the 'fifties. Beginning as the extraordinary 'Crescent' and coming fully into use in 1851, it was again a product of Lewis Cubitt's fertile and original thinking, (see of course Top Shed, by its chief in BR days, P.N.Townend, Ian Allan, and more recently Great Northern Engine Sheds, Griffiths and Hooper, Irwell Press 1989) though as originally drawn up it was not to the precise requirements of the Great Northern's Edward Bury, who promptly re-designed it. It was busy from the first, beginning a long history of overcrowding and running to catch up with developments. As early as 8th November 1851 Sturrock held forth: 'To work our line, I estimate on the opening to London by Messrs. Cubitt Mowatt Denniston [spelling of names varies in the GN Minutes] and myself .. that we would have to run 55,680 miles per week which would require 34 Passenger Engines and 44 Goods Engines in steam daily. Has now sometimes reached 80,000 miles per week and with the Exhibition Excursions we reached 83,076 miles in one week'.(!)

(National Railway Museum)

Amusing comparisons were highly popular on the pre-War companies especially the 'David and Goliath' sort. No. 7 Typhoon is one of the Romney Hythe and Dymchurch engines, based upon the Gresley Pacifics. Top shed 1927.

(The Thompson Society)

Dominion of Canada in the Kings Cross gloaming.

(Alec Swain Coll.)

The hazards of engine labouring: (i)gravity and (ii) (see inset) hot metal – note the cloth on our bowler hatted cleaner's left wrist.
(Alec Swain Coll.)

Kings Cross early on was modernised with mechanical coaling plant, completed towards the end of 1932. The company described it thus: The reconstruction of King's Cross Locomotive Depot has been in hand for several months, and a concrete mixer, stacks of bricks and other paraphernalia of the Engineer's Department occupy a prominent place. The scheme is very comprehensive and includes the conversion of the carriage repair shop into a locomotive shed, the improvement of the layout of the yard with additional roads, the provision of wet ash pits, larger turntable, additional wheel drop and numerous other alterations such as the adoption of electrical energy, improvements to the sand and water supplied &c. *The old roundhouse was demolished some time ago. Beyond York Way (note the ramp down into the yard on the left and also the 'Ebonite Tower') lies the North London Railway bridge and partly obscured by the coaling tower the Funeral station, latterly a clothing store. The view is particularly useful to show how closely the mpd rubbed shoulders with the goods and mineral lines either side. The problems of the pilots in clear weather, let alone on foggy nights where all those lines came together will be appreciated.*

(National Railway Museum)

Engines at Kings Cross around 1960. The modernisation did not render operations wholly as convenient as might be; the sand hopper for instance was inconveniently sited for peak times and hand buckets remained in use to the end. This was a particular problem with the A4s, the stuff easily spilling onto the valve gear.

(Alec Swain)

4489, made ready for some major task no doubt, hurries the onset of dark with its own outpourings.

(Alec Swain Coll.)

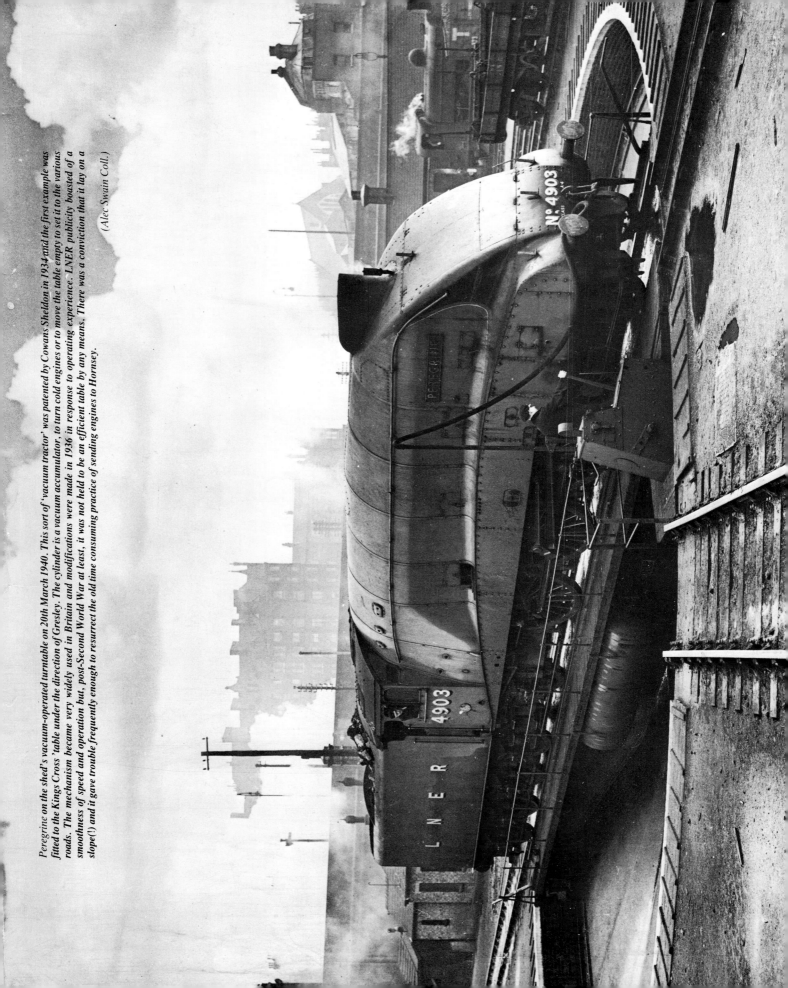

Peregrine on the shed's vacuum-operated turntable on 20th March 1940. This sort of 'vacuum tractor' was patented by Cowans Sheldon in 1934 and the first example was fitted to the Kings Cross 'table under the direction of Gresley. The cylinder is a vacuum accumulator, to turn cold engines or to move the table empty to set it to the various roads. The mechanism became very widely used in Britain and modifications were made in 1936 in response to operating experience. LNER publicity boasted of a smoothness of speed and operation but, post-Second World War at least, it was not held to be an efficient table by any means. There was a conviction that it lay on a slope(!) and it gave trouble frequently enough to resurrect the old time consuming practice of sending engines to Hornsey.

(Alec Swain Coll.)

The great bulk of the Kings Cross 'Cenotaph' one of the few, surely, to feature (blink and you miss it) on film, in the The Ladykillers. *The comedy is quite lovely and is well worth watching for bits of the whole Kings Cross area, including Copenhagen Tunnel and what looks like Camley Street — the coal drops incidentally also feature in the opening shots of Alfie.*

(Alec Swain Coll.)

Rerailing demo in the shed yard, on 31st May 1956.

(National Railway Museum)

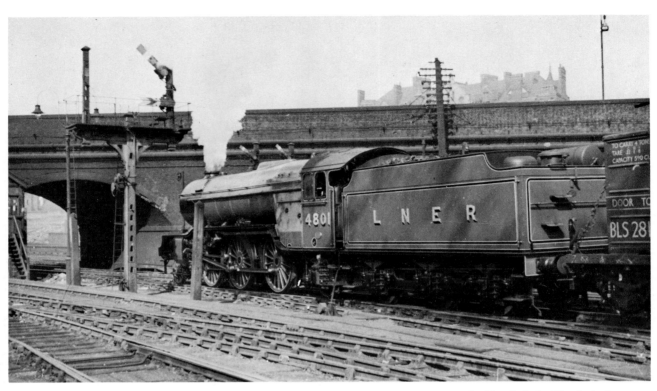

V2 2-6-2 No. 4801, new in April 1938, about to leave with what looks like the 3.40pm Scotch Goods. Close by is the 'Five Arches' signalbox, which had windows in a bay formation on its left hand side, to allow the levers to be pulled.

(A.B. Collins Coll.)

5.52 p.m. Cambridge and Peterbrough train leaving north end of Copenhagen Tunnel, under the skew bridge, behind B1 4-6-0s 61138 and 61121, on 14th July 1954. The train split at Hitchin; 61138 would take the Peterborough portion, 61121 the Cambridge.

(Brian Morrison)

The non-stop blasting from Copenhagen Tunnel on 11th July 1953.

(Brian Morrison)

Light engines, coupled together for convenience, about to plunge into Gas Works Tunnel.

(A.B.Collins Coll.)

Cock o'the North **under the North London Railway bridge. First trips by 2001 to London were on 11th – 16th June 1934, due in the terminus at 4.15pm. Later visits included the dynamometer car, which is not present here.**

(A.B.Collins Coll.)

Varied scene at Belle Isle. This is the B3 No. 6169 Lord Faringdon, *an engine of Great Central origin. The class worked out of Kings Cross (*The RCTS *History declares it 'difficult to see the history of these engines as a success story ...) with 'patchy' results in the middle part of the 1920s.*

(A.B.Collins Coll.)

The cauldron between the Kings Cross tunnels, a vast smoke wreathed pit that, despite the constant sulphureous outpourings, was far from some dead, blasted heath. Every bit of bank was waving grass in summer (patches of lupins, for some reason, dotted the edges of the GN main line) and birdsong floated across these caverns in moments of calm. These could be short lived of course and moments of drama in the place naturally linger more forcefully in the mind. Colin Walker, well known for work at this site has written about the effect on one's nerves, 'a quite overwhelming experience'. Brian Morrison and others have similar tales. More eerie and startling still after all this could be the sudden clonk of a signal arm.

(A.B.Collins Coll.)

Descending Holloway Bank, B1 No.61223 on an up Cambridge excursion, on 17th May 1961.
(Brian Morrison)

V2 60854 on a Newcastle express, 17th May 1961.

(Brian Morrison)

N7 0-6-2T with down ecs, on 24th July 1958.

(Brian Morrison)

'The Elizabethan' above, in the hands of Golden Fleece, *and below* St. Simon *on the 7.15pm for Aberdeen, on 5th July 1952.*
(Brian Morrison)

Latter Days

Weeks from the commencement of the British Railways *Modernization Plan* in 1955 long cherished ideas for the remodelling of Kings Cross station surfaced — 'rebuilding wholly or in part and complete replacing of its approaches'. Kings Cross and Hornsey sheds, it was envisaged, would be reconstructed for the 'new form of motive power' (diesel *and electric*) and 'new depots for the maintenance of main line coaching stock and multiple unit suburban trains' would be built. Much of this did come to pass, but hardly in the fashion envisaged.

By 1957 the Kings Cross A4 stud was being diluted, by A3s and A1s, to an extent not seen before, for the streamlined Pacifics were proving increasingly heavy on maintenance. Steam of course still abounded, with the occasional Haymarket 'stranger' to enliven things but the diesels were coming and a two car set, ominously, underwent ATC tests between Grantham and Kings Cross. A London Midland unit, Nos. 79128 and 79683, it started out from Derby works on the first Monday morning in February 1958. For three weeks it left Grantham at 10.45am on weekdays, creeping into Kings Cross and its pall of locomotive smoke at 1.14pm and 're-turning north on a 120 minute timing to Grantham'. D201, a new 2000hp EE Type 4 (the first, D200, had been unveiled to much trumpeting at Norwich on April 18th) arrived at Hornsey on April 26th in preparation for a crew training trip. By the end of the month it was back at Doncaster works for remedial attention. In those dozing days as the 'fifties passed steam still seemed long secure and the visit of a Scottish A3 to The Cross, *Spion Kop* on the Easter Monday was considered more noteworthy.

D201 soon returned and ran a Sheffield trip, with six Pullmans (under some secrecy apparently) on 29th April. It was a historic working, though 15 minutes late and revealed (reportedly) disappointing acceleration abilities. Throughout June it was backwards and forwards on various trials, tests and training workings. Confidence grew and on June 21st it worked the down *Flying Scotsman* to Newcastle....

There was little concept then of the rate of change, at least among the onlooking public;* the Great Northern main line was only now being surveyed, in apparently desultory fashion, for electrification which never came and A3s were being altered, with trough deflectors and double chimneys. Drastic change seemed comfortably remote.

G.F.Fiennes, Line Traffic Manager of the GN Section revealed intentions to the Rotary Clubs of Stevenage and Hitchin in June 1958. The GN line services would be the smartest in the world, beginning with a new dieselised passenger service on the Hertford Loop in January 1959, together with a better steam service upon completion of the Hadley Wood widening in the summer of 1958.** Electrification would somehow flow from this, to be fully operational by 1964...

Though not apparently among BR management — witness Fiennes' optimistic prediction of electrification.
**In the event not finalised until May 1959.*

The Pacifics' successors. The peculiar 'Golden fing' was a startling sight to those of us used to the more restrained headboards of the steam era but the Deltics, even allowing for our early prejudice, made for a fine sight in their dashing livery. The subsequent popularity of these big diesels was a contrast to our typical urchin's reaction in 1961 — then they were shunned. There was some disapointment, nay, mystification I seem to recall, that they were not painted 'like the blue one'. Allan Baker, who operated the locos out of the gleaming new depot at Finsbury Park (see the excellent Deltics at Work, *Baker & Morrison, Ian Allan, 1985) has pointed to the astonishing mileages the introduction of the big 'Type 5s', brought, working 'the first true cyclic diagrams'. They roared and whined and blasted their way in and out of Kings Cross for nearly two decades, and were particularly impressive screeching and throbbing around the groaning curves of 'the passenger loco', given over to diesels with the construction of a proper servicing shed, a facility which had been denied steam. The awesome twin blasts of exhaust were almost thrilling, in a less environmentally — conscious age, rocketing up and outwards to signal the issuing forth of yet another monster from the yard.*

(Brian Morrison)

D206 arrived at Hornsey at the end of July 1958, slotting unobtrusively into the crew training jobs of its accomplice, D201. From the winter timetable of September 15th five intensive weekly rosters began with only five of the Type 4s, booked for 4,500 miles a week each…'the first real British test of all the advertised benefits of intensive use over long distances of a stud of standard units.' Full implementation was delayed until 29th September … 'pending delivery of the fifth unit.'

Type 2 diesels for freight and passenger work were also soon being delivered to Hornsey and Birmingham RC&W Co. D5300 made its debut on Hertford passenger turns in September 1958. Diesel performance generally was 'less than impeccable' but the Sheffield Pullman trains were something of a flagship and every effort was made to preserve Type 4 haulage of *The Master Cutler*. In the autumn and winter of 1958 many trials and much exasperation was endured and despite the worryingly frequent ignominy of multiple failures, usually it seemed, ending behind a scruffy B1, 90 minutes late or whatever, the D200 programme of 1958 was a bold one, with perilously meagre resources.

Deltic arrived in January 1959 and though out of action at Hornsey in May it was soon back on regular Kings Cross — Doncaster jobs. Most of the EE 'Baby Deltics' reached Hornsey by the end of May but nerves were frayed and hopes faltering badly by the summer of 1959. The BRCW locos had piston troubles and spare dmu sets from country districts were being requisitioned, some of their home jobs reverting to steam. *Trains Illustrated* in October reported that a Kings Cross steam locomotive was prepared as stand by for every one of the Type 4 duties. Though there could have been few things worse for a BR engineer to hear, in the trough of teething troubles this long lamented journal followed with the devastating and fascinating point that *in such a situation there will be many who will wonder whether the construction of new boilers to save the double chimney A3s from extinction might not be a worthwhile investment — particularly as there is evidence that the much more youthful — and nominally class 8 A1s are beginning to promise more trouble than the Gresley Pacifics ever did at the same age, whereas the class 7 double chimney A3s have become the apple of every East Coast Route shedmaster's eye and are used on the most exacting workings the line has to offer.* In the event twenty new diagram 107 boilers were put onto A4s and A3s from July 1959 to July 1961.

Brush Type 2s (class 31), D5563 and D5564 turned up at Hornsey on November 20th 1959 for trials, considered more suitable, through reasons of power, on such workings as Kings Cross — Peterborough. They were to prove a success and the BRCW/Sulzer and NB Type 2s went to Scotland. The first A3 Pacific was condemned at the end of 1959, *Solario* with a cracked frame. Traction changes at Kings Cross from hereon would be extraordinary. Brush Type 2s *in multiple* worked the *Heart of Midlothian* and *Northumbrian* in February/March 1960. The first through diesel working Kings Cross — Edinburgh came in 1960, a Type 4 on the 'Car Sleeper'; Britannias displaced from the GE were an unexpected development, working from Immingham on Cleethorpes trains but Finsbury Park (Clarence Yard) diesel depot had opened in April 1960. Diesels were bearing its shed code 34G and the lifeblood of Top Shed was inexorably flowing away to 'The Park'. The first production series Deltic, D9001, arrived in London in January 1961 for an exhibition at Stratford and Type 2s of a different make (but destined to be relatively short lived on workings out of the terminus) also date from about this period, Sulzers in the D5000 series from GE line depots. The district maintained its reputation for surprises and despite the closure of Hatfield shed amidst weekly arrivals of diesels exotic steam instances could be found — an LMR Jubilee, O1 2-8-0s, a K2 No. 61756 and a Q1 No. 33002

at Haringay. The Deltics now began their prodigious mileage feats, Haymarket examples bringing up the morning *Talisman* to work back with *The Aberdonian* and so on.

The great event was to be the new winter timetable of 1961, 'to restore the highest pre-war standards of express passenger train speed between London and the West Riding, Newcastle and Edinburgh…' Delays, and problems meant only a proportion of the order of 22 Deltics was available and only a tenth of the accelerations were possible. Moreover crucial reconstruction work, especially the easing of the Peterborough curves, was in abeyance on the instruction of the Ministry of Transport. It was a bit of a mess, and derived principally from the halt to electrification plans. As *Trains Illustrated* put it, in rather frustrated but anonymous tone in 1961: *what we now have is a comparatively hurried extemporisation forced on the East Coast Route by the abandonment of electrification, even though at the time the decision was taken there was not available a high powered British diesel engine or locomotive complete, which was sufficiently proved for mass production, so that the East Coast Route could still provide something like the service envisaged with electric traction.*

In contrast to these early trials and tribulations, by 1963 with EE Type 3 and 4 (class 37 and 40), Peaks (class 45etc) and Deltics, there seemed to be diesels galore: D1500 in a debut heavily redolent of symbolism, displaced *Mallard* on October 8th 1962, on the 5.23pm Doncaster train.

The end of steam at Kings Cross was not greatly heralded, probably because it was still commonplace across much of the country; the *Railway Magazine* reported June 15th 1963 as the last day and the *Railway Observer* the next day, the 16th. This was 60158 *Aberdonian*, on the 10.45pm Leeds train. 'Top Shed' closed that day but the engines proved persistent. Pacifics were still turning up as substitutes and on freight (apparently the Top Shed coaling plant was surreptitiously topped up) through the summer. A1 and A3 Pacifics, V2s, 9Fs and B1s all turned up for failed diesels, into November 1963. *Silver Fox* worked a Leeds train on October 29th, despite 'its withdrawal nine days earlier'.

What followed was demonstrably the Deltic era, in which Kings Cross took on an almost unique air amongst the great railway stations of Britain, or at least the capital. The Cross was amongst the most 'active' to be found. There remained a marvellous variety for a start — the colossal Deltics, the boxlike and rumbling Brush Type 2s, whistling class 40s, Peaks from the North East, handsome 47s and others, as well as clattering, fussy dmu sets, lurching and careering between the platforms and the tunnels. A ghastly 'sixties redevelopment proposal floundered but a new concourse in the early 1970s was hardly more uplifting; fighting your way through threading, ill-tempered queues, it was nevertheless still possible to soak in the echoing spaces of the train shed, still blasted by locomotive noise, and the contrasting muffled nooks and crannies of the suburban side. The diesels still followed, essentially, steam practice, running out light to reverse twice into the old servicing area. This was now equipped with diesel examination shed and refuelling tanks and every one of the frequent movements was accomplished to much shrieking and throbbing. The sudden plumes of exhaust, though a ghastly blue polluting oil mist, were a startling sight and now missed, despite the 'green' considerations.

All this changed with electrification and the introduction of high speed trains. Many of the suburban trains were got rid of, diverted to the Northern City line to Moorgate, overhead supports first appearing at Gas Works Tunnel around June 1976. The first stage of the £63M scheme, the inner suburban, was inaugurated in November 1976, despite shortages and a lack of experience with ultra-tight station stops and procedures. 46 of the eventual 64 class 313 units were to have been available for the inner suburban service and on the big day, only 28 units, the operating minimum, were ready.

Opprobrium followed, as surely as night comes after day, but it was nevertheless a remarkable staff effort — see in particular Ford's article in *Modern Railways* of September 1977. The full electric timetable Kings Cross — Royston came in February 1978 with the main line station energised in August the previous year. The new route to Moorgate had been commissioned with the earlier inner suburban schemes, so that the station could be remodelled, its principal effect the abandonment of the eastern Gas Works and Copenhagen bores and the Hotel and York Road curves. The track layout, known as 'the Throat' was remodelled and resignalled from January to April 1977, the final stage of a project involving over 80 route miles. The up slow was taken across a renewed Holloway skew into the western Gas Works and Copenhagen tunnels and the eastern bores abandoned. All four remaining tracks in the Gas Works tunnels were put over to two way working. This was apparently influenced (in part at least) by an outstanding, though dropped, proposal to use the eastern Copenhagen bore for the erstwhile Third London Airport trains. These were to run from a new junction at Haringay, running up to the eastern tunnel and then swing over on a new bridge into a proper terminal in Kings Cross goods yard. In the 1970s these ideas were still borne in mind and they have echoes in the new proposals for the Channel Tunnel. Five platforms were abandoned, the old ones on the 'local' side and various alterations made to those remaining.

HST sets (of class 254) began their upgraded work with the May 1978 timetable, allowing perhaps the greatest and most sustained impact on journey times ever. There were the usual delays, late deliveries and technical hitches, compounded by a Government decision to curtail the number of sets involved. The 1980s thereafter began the High Speed Train decade at The Cross, the snaking sets hurrying in and out with formidable efficiency. With them, the electrics and the remodelling, the station lost its confused, rushing air; dereliction set in to either side and the various abandoned tunnels gape in rubbish strewn reproof of modern development. With full mainline electric working the station waits now in anticipation of 'International Passenger Terminal' developments to come. Its trains are modern and sealed and the circulation area as anonymous as a motorway service station but walk outwards to the well of light at the end of Cubitt's screen; in the yellow bricks, the shadows and archways, the curves and still-oddly deserted corners, the Great station, of Atlantics, Pacifics and Deltics, waits still…

D206 arrives with 'The Master Cutler', a train tailored for the new diesels, on 7th October 1958. D206 had joined its fellow D201 towards the end of July and through the 1960s in particlar the whistling progress and crashing gait of these vast machines (the huge bogies raised particular protest from the long–suffering points about the engine yard) characterised The Cross post–steam as much, perhaps, as the Deltics. The passing of the class 40s, with an engineering lineage traceable directly to late 1940s, is a sobering thought, a last tenuous link with the time before Nationalisation and a measure of continuing progress and evolution.

(Railway Covers)

The North London viaduct, with trackwork much like earlier times, but well into the 'blue era', 15th July 1975. The Deltic is Meld on a Newcastle train, viewed from close by the Ladykiller's lair.

(John Glover)

Unidentified class 45 with an up semi fast from Leeds, on 27th July 1979. The photograph is remarkable for several features; (i)the new electric railway; Introduction of the full Outer-Suburban electric service on Monday 6th February 1978 between Royston (Hertfordshire) and London King's Cross heralds a new era in suburban rail transport – the virtual completion of British Rail's £66M Great Northern Suburban electrification scheme. Only a few minor tidying-up jobs remain to be completed. (from BR's Livewire Progress Report No. 12). (ii)the class 45 'Peak' diesels have come and gone and are now long extinct on the GN. (iii)the diesel shed itself has fallen out use and is now no more. (iv)through all this roller coaster change the old goods buildings of the 1850s still stare blankly out, yards away and worlds apart.

(John Glover)

The eastern Gas Works bore now abandoned, class 43 DVT power car No. 43068 emerges into the terminus, on 12th August 1989, heading the 14.10 Leeds-Kings Cross with class 91 No. 91003, which is propelling the train, still in the tunnel. By the tunnel mouth awaiting its next turn of duty is class 47/4 No. 47539 Rochdale Pioneers. *Now The Cross had seen some funny names over the years — Merry Hampton, Pretty Polly and St Paddy,* **but** Rochdale Pioneers?

(Brian Morrison)

Busy time at Kings Cross on 31st August 1989. From left to right are: 91004 on arrival with the 12.10 ex-Leeds, 91009 on the 15.10 to Leeds, 43156 leading the 15.00 to Glasgow Queen Street and 47626 (retaining GWR-stye Atlas plates with Mainline livery) awaiting departure time with the 15.13 parcels to Newcastle.

(Brian Morrison)

Hauling Intercity Charter stock instead of the usual Mk.3s and DVT, class 89 No. 89001 Avocet *awaits the 17.36 departure for Peterborough, on the evening of 17th February 1989. In the adjacent platforms, Intercity 125 stock forms services for Hull, Glasgow and Bradford, led by power cars Nos. 43197, 43074 and 43121.*

(*Brian Morrison*)

Old and New orders at Kings Cross on 24th November 1989. Headed by class 43 power car No. 43077 and class 91 No. 91009, the 19.00 and 19.30 InterCity services to Newcastle and Leeds, respectively, await their alloted moment to power away into the night. Some things never change, and this is only the latest in long years of contrast and change at The Cross.

(Brian Morrison)

Tailpiece. 'With one mighty bound …' powering under the Regents Canal engines fought free of the cauldron, its tracks and smoke and tunnels, and the suburbs, 'Northern Heights' and the East Coast main line beckoned. After this the line became a more 'ordinary' railway and though wonders of a different kind would be encountered nothing could quite match the tracks and tunnels of The Cross.

This book is for dear Joybells, who would have smiled at some of the Copenhagen Street bits.

A Note.

I first knew Kings Cross, a place of great wonder, as small child in the 1950s. Fear and fascination in the sort of childhood mix never really lost to the memory filled me on that vast iron bridge, and the crashing, rolling echoes and smoke of that cavernous place was the highlight of Sunday mornings out with 'me Dad'. Countless subsequent visits, loose of parental eyes reinforced my attachment to this rambling building, a fondness which has stayed through a lifetime. Pacifics in joyful profusion (for long I was too young or dim to divine the reasons for them being the same engines we saw at New Southgate – should'nt they be *different*, that is, *new ones?*) gave way to diesels which the platform end urchin culture at first loftily rejected. In any case Saturday jobs and advancing years were bringing economic freedoms, and the chance to visit more exotic climes, Feltham or even Watford.

This is not meant to be a thoroughly comprehensive history of Kings Cross – there never has been and probably never will, for a weighty volume(s) indeed will be needed for that. This account however does bring to light a number of photographs and diagrams, most of them hitherto little known and draws upon a number of Great Northern, LNER and Board of Trade Minutes and Reports. Through these some of the points I hope will have an original air to them. The text dwells variously upon 'ancient history', the 1930s, the War and the following BR steam era, the dieselisation and thwarted electrification of the 1960s, ending with the final triumph of the electrics from the 1970s to the present day. In between are some snippets of social history, derived from family legend and no doubt impossibly biased.

For Kings Cross there are many published sources, variously harnessed for this first *Great British Station*. Gairns' *Notable Railway Stations and their Traffic* of 1914 is enlightening but amongst the best accounts so far has probably been Johns in 1952: *Railway Magazine, One Hundred Years at Kings Cross*, upon which most accounts seem to have drawn. This was the year of the station's Centenary of course and probably the best rendering since has been by Jackson, in the memorable *London's Termini*. *Traffic Improvements at Kings Cross*, anon, from the 1920s is required reading, as are the various 'insider' accounts, by Medcalf and to a lesser extent other GN officers. *King's Cross in the Twenties*, Oakwood 1978, by W. Rayner Thrower is a lovely read. Snippets from all the journals are always of enormous value though in the last few decades they amount to an almost unwieldy quantity. This account leans, photographically at least, most heavily upon the 1930s and the BR steam period. I make no apology for this; such an emphasis more or less reflects the material available and, more compellingly, it celebrates my personal recollection, the 'fifties and 'sixties as a lad and the 1930s as family folk memory. It also leaves room for an effort more firmly rooted in Great Northern times and will even, with luck, encourage such a project on the part of some stalwart. This might require, as intimated above, several volumes and one hardly dares hope that enough photographs exist for the GN period. Not that those thirsting for early detail should be disappointed over much. The GN Directors believed brevity a virtue in the consigning of their deliberations to posterity, and most of what there is from the late 1840s/early 1850s period, as it relates to Kings Cross, lies within. This account I hope provides an episodic summary of the development of The Cross, more than a potted history but far from the last word. Kings Cross still is one of the *Great British Stations* and will remain so – I hope these pages will reveal a little at least of exactly how that greatness came about, how it was maintained and nurtured, and how the fascination of its earlier (and middle) years can endure.

It remains to acknowledge the kindness and help of several people; the book was completed under the guidance and stern reproof of Willie Yeadon, John Aylard and Bert Collins. I am grateful to all three for their time and effort, and for many previously unsuspected insights into the LNER. Whilst the book owes much to the particular knowledge of these gentlemen I reserve blame (and worse) for the opinions expressed and ideas presented (I suspect in one or two instances I was a less than perfect pupil). I would also like to thank Alec Swain for the loan of a number of photographs, John and Christine, George and Beverly and especially Wendy, who apart from everything else more than compensated for my as yet (though I fear it will long remain so) rudimentary word processing skills.